SMITHSON

T0182406

BRAIN BOOSTER
HUMAN BODY

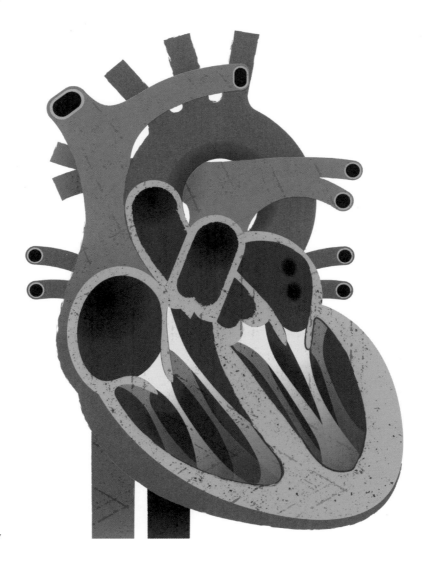

Previously published as
Active Learning: Human Body

Project Art Editor Jessica Tapolcai
Designers Annabel Schick, Gilda Pacitti, Vicky Read, Laura Gardner Design Studio
Senior Editors Satu Hämeenaho-Fox, Rebecca Fry
Editors Ashwin Khurana, Sophie Adam, Lizzie Munsey
US Editor Heather Wilcox
Editorial Assistant Elise Solberg
Managing Editor Carine Tracanelli
Managing Art Editor Anna Hall
Jacket Designer Stephanie Tan
Jacket Design Development Manager Sophia MTT
Production Editor Gill Reid
Production Controller Poppy David
Art Director Karen Self
Publisher Andrew Macintyre
Publishing Director Jonathan Metcalf

Illustrators Mark Ruffle, Mark Clifton, Dan Crisp, Gus Scott

Previously published in 2023 as
Active Learning: Human Body
This American Edition, 2024
Published in the United States by DK Publishing
1745 Broadway, 20th Floor, New York, NY 10019

Copyright © 2023, 2024 Dorling Kindersley Limited
DK, a Division of Penguin Random House LLC
24 25 26 27 28 10 9 8 7 6 5 4 3 2 1
001–343227–Sep/2024

A catalog record for this book
is available from the Library of Congress.
ISBN 978-0-5938-4797-8

Printed and bound in China

www.dk.com

MIX
Paper | Supporting responsible forestry
FSC™ C018179

This book was made with Forest Stewardship Council™ certified paper – one small step in DK's commitment to a sustainable future. Learn more at **www.dk.com/uk/information/sustainability**

THE AUTHORS AND CONSULTANT

Shari Last is an author and editor who has contributed to many bestselling reference and activity books for children. She writes on a wide variety of topics, from nature and science to LEGO® and Star Wars™, and enjoys making learning fun.

Rebecca Fry has spent more than 25 years in illustrated reference as an editor and a writer. She has a BSc in Anthropology from UCL, where her love of writing unambiguous nonfiction text was born.

Dr. Kristina Routh is a medical doctor and qualified specialist in Public Health Medicine with more than 20 years' experience as a medical consultant on books covering all aspects of health and the human body.

CONTENTS

BUILDING BLOCKS

Our bodies are made up of nearly 40 trillion tiny building blocks called cells. Similar cells group together to form tissue, such as fat, muscle, bone, nerves, and blood. Tissues group together to form organs. And organs make up the systems that keep our bodies alive and well. Cells might be tiny, but they all play an important part in the functioning of our bodies.

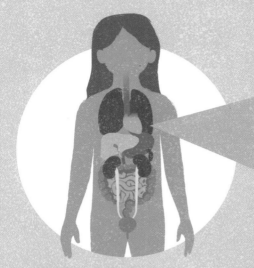

1 Organ system
A system is a collection of organs that carries out one of the body's crucial tasks. There are 11 organ systems in the human body.

What's in a cell?
Cells come in all shapes and sizes, depending on their function and which tissue or organ they belong to. Whatever shape they are, most cells have the same tiny structures (called organelles) inside, which do certain jobs.

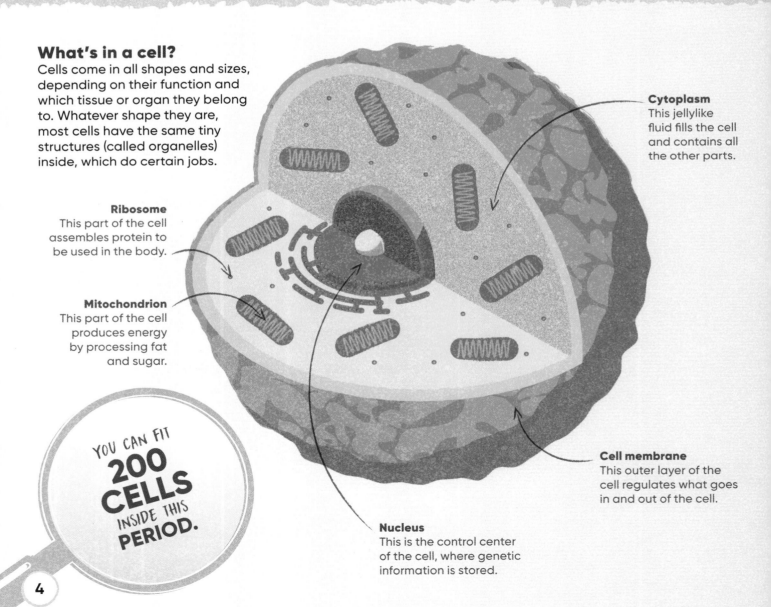

Cytoplasm
This jellylike fluid fills the cell and contains all the other parts.

Ribosome
This part of the cell assembles protein to be used in the body.

Mitochondrion
This part of the cell produces energy by processing fat and sugar.

Cell membrane
This outer layer of the cell regulates what goes in and out of the cell.

Nucleus
This is the control center of the cell, where genetic information is stored.

YOU CAN FIT
200 CELLS
INSIDE THIS **PERIOD.**

4

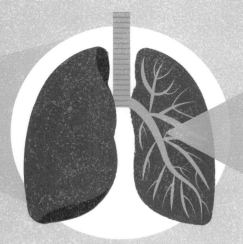

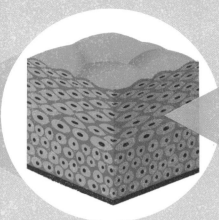

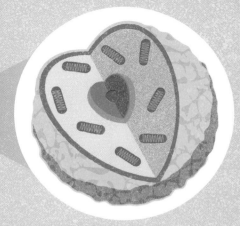

2 Organ
Organs are parts of the body that carry out a specific function. The lungs, for example, put oxygen into our blood when we breathe.

3 Tissue
Groups of similar cells form tissue. Tissue is the material that makes up all parts of the body, from bones to organs.

4 Cell
Cells are the building blocks of the human body. They have different features to carry out their own special jobs.

LABEL THE BODY PARTS
Write the correct label next to these pictures of a **cell**, **tissue**, **organ**, and **organ system**.

a ....

b ....

c ....

d ....

WRITE IT!

MATCH THE CELL TYPES
Can you match each of these cell types to the correct description?

MATCH IT!

a

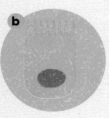

b

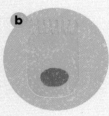

c

Fat cell
Big and round for storing lots of fat

Nerve cell
A long body and short, spiky arms

Intestine cell
A frilly edge to absorb nutrients

Muscle cell
Long and thin, but can shorten to create movement

White blood cell
Disease-fighting cell with bumpy appearance

Red blood cell
Round and red with a curved surface and no nucleus

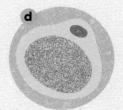

d

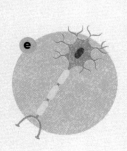

e

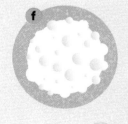

f

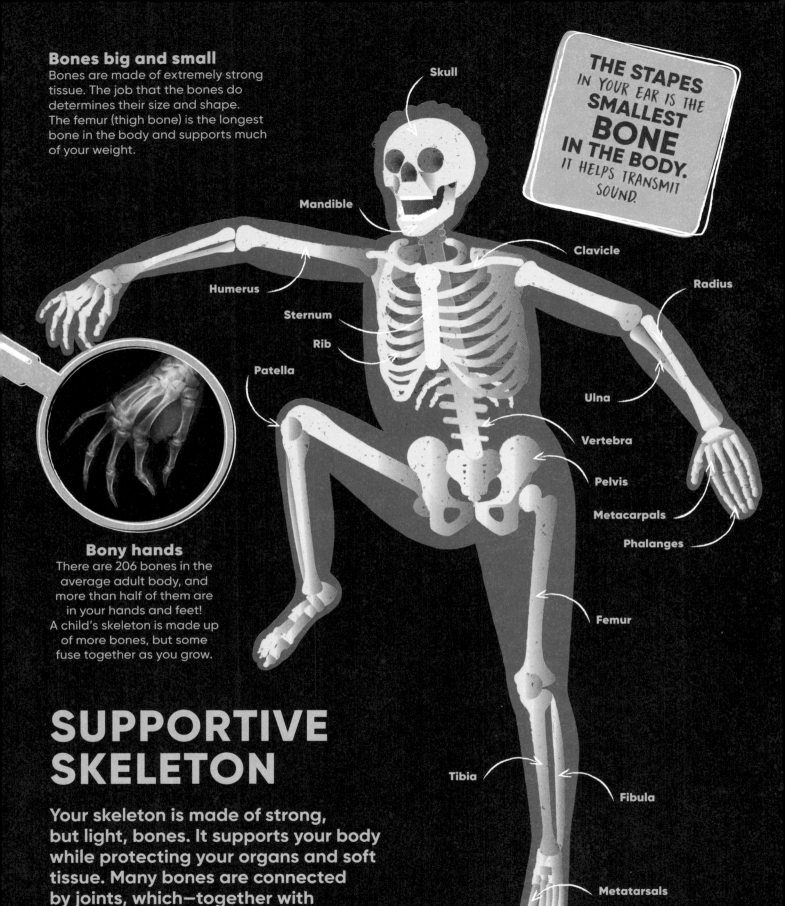

Bones big and small

Bones are made of extremely strong tissue. The job that the bones do determines their size and shape. The femur (thigh bone) is the longest bone in the body and supports much of your weight.

THE STAPES IN YOUR EAR IS THE **SMALLEST BONE IN THE BODY.** IT HELPS TRANSMIT SOUND.

Skull

Mandible

Humerus

Sternum

Rib

Patella

Clavicle

Radius

Ulna

Vertebra

Pelvis

Metacarpals

Phalanges

Femur

Tibia

Fibula

Metatarsals

Phalanges

Bony hands

There are 206 bones in the average adult body, and more than half of them are in your hands and feet! A child's skeleton is made up of more bones, but some fuse together as you grow.

SUPPORTIVE SKELETON

Your skeleton is made of strong, but light, bones. It supports your body while protecting your organs and soft tissue. Many bones are connected by joints, which—together with muscles—allow the body to move.

COMPLETE THE SKELETON

Follow these instructions to complete the body.

1. Draw in the other halves of the skull and pelvis.

2. The five bones on the tray below are missing from the body. Decide where each should go and then draw it in the correct place on the skeleton.

FILL ME IN!

a ....

b ....

c ....

d ....

e ....

WRITE IT!

LABEL THE BONES

Use the words from the word box to label your completed skeleton.

Vertebra

Clavicle

Rib

Humerus

Femur

UNSCRAMBLE THE WORD

Cross out the letters of the word "skeleton" and then unscramble the ones that are left to find the name of the longest bone in the human body.

O E L U T E N F K R S
M   E

_ _ _ _ _

WHAT CAN YOU SEE?

X-rays allow us to take photos of the bones inside our bodies. The X-rays on the right show some of the bones in the word box below. Circle the bones that you can see.

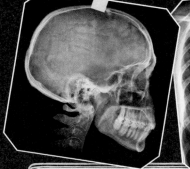
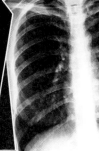

FIND IT!

| Ribs | Pelvis | Femur | Patella |
| Metatarsals | Skull | Tibia | Mandible |

INSIDE A BONE

Bones provide structural support to your body but also function as organs, with a blood supply and nerves. There are layers of different types of tissue. The outer part is dense, but inner parts are lighter and less dense, with a honeycomb-like structure. Our bones are incredibly strong, yet light enough for us to move around easily.

BONE MARROW CAN MAKE AROUND **2 MILLION** BLOOD CELLS EVERY SECOND!

Bone anatomy
Each layer of tissue inside a bone has its own purpose—from the tough, protective outer layers, all the way to the inner section that houses bone marrow. Let's take a peek inside a bone and discover what each part does.

Blood vessels
Veins and arteries transport blood to and from the bone.

Spongy bone
Honeycomb-like tissue helps keep bones light.

Periosteum
A hard fiber covers the whole bone surface.

Red bone marrow
This soft tissue manufactures blood cells.

Compact bone
This dense, hard tissue makes bones strong.

THE PRIMARY JOB OF SOME **BONE CELLS** IS TO **CREATE NEW** BONE CELLS.

LABEL THE TISSUE
Look at these magnified bone cross sections and use the words below to label the different types of tissue found in bones.

Spongy bone

Red bone marrow

Compact bone

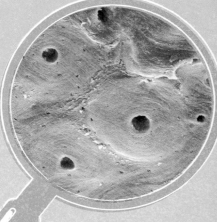

a ....

....

MATCH THE STAGES

Over time, a baby's bones grow longer and change from cartilage—a tough but flexible tissue—into solid bone. Cartilage cells group together, and then calcium and other minerals attach to them, turning them into bone. New blood vessels and more bone tissue continue to grow. Can you match the different stages of bone growth to the pictures?

MATCH IT!

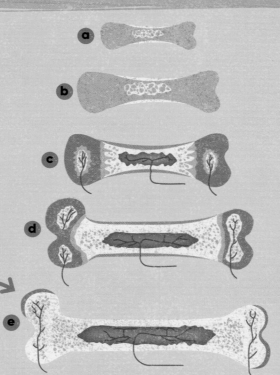

Adult
Bone is fully formed, and the cells are constantly remodeling the bone.

Embryo
Bone cells start to form within cartilage structures.

Teenager
Bone grows bigger and stronger as the remaining cartilage turns to bone.

Child
Blood vessels and bone marrow form within the bone.

Newborn baby
More of the cartilage turns to bone.

COLOR THE BONE

Use what you've learned about the unique structure of bone to help you complete the diagram, using colors from the key below.

1 Red bone marrow
2 Compact bone
3 Spongy bone
4 Periosteum

COLOR IT!

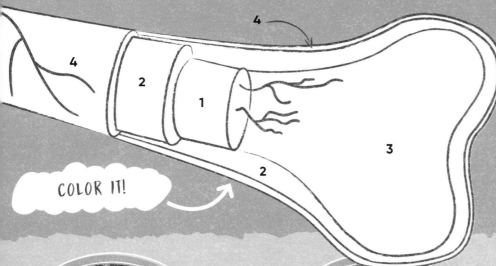

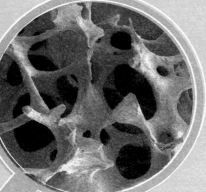

DECODE IT!

Which type of cells are produced by bone marrow? To find the answer, cross out the letters of the word "bone" and then unscramble the remaining letters.

D N O L E O S B E L O C L B

_ _ _ _ _   _ _ _ _ _

b ....

....

c ....

....

Types of joint

From bending or reaching to jumping or climbing, your body moves in many different ways. Here are the most common types of joint.

Pivot joint
A peglike part of one bone fits into a ring-shaped part of another bone. This allows for a rotating movement.

Gliding joint
The flat surfaces of two bones glide over one another, allowing for some limited movement in all directions.

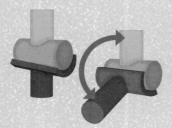

Hinge joint
A rounded bone fits into a concave bone, like a hinge. This allows for movement forward and backward, but not from side to side.

Ball-and-socket joint
A ball-shaped bone fits into the socket of another bone. This allows for a wide range of movement in all directions.

Ellipsoidal joint
Like a ball-and-socket joint but with an elliptical (oval) shape, this joint allows for side-to-side movement in many directions. It is more limited than a ball-and-socket joint.

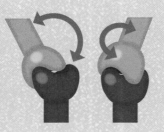

Saddle joint
Saddle-shaped bones can move over one another forward, backward, and from side to side, but their shape restricts rotating movements.

JOINTS

The place where two bones meet is called a joint. There are various types of joint in your body, and each of them allows for a specific kind of movement. Think about it: Running is a very different movement than waving.

FIND THE JOINTS
Can you find all six types of joint from the panel in the wordsearch below?

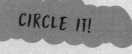
CIRCLE IT!

```
C D L J F G B I D D S
A E M N O P A R M N O
L B L E F G L O D E F
E L A N O P L R M N O
L C D E F G A I D E F
I H I N G E N R M N O
P C O E S A D D L E F
D C S E F G S P D D F
S L P I P S O I D A L
A C I E F G C V D E F
I A L N O P K O M N O
L K L E F G E T D E F
F L E I P I T L I B A
A G N I D I L G P I O
```

Hinge	Gliding	Pivot
Ellipsoidal	Ball-and-socket	Saddle

TAKE A LOOK INSIDE

Bones don't rub against each other within a joint—that would hurt! The ends of the bones are covered by smooth tissue called cartilage. Surrounding this is synovial fluid, a thick liquid made by the synovial membrane. All of this is encased in a protective capsule and surrounded by tough, stretchy ligaments. Color in the diagram to show the different parts of a joint.

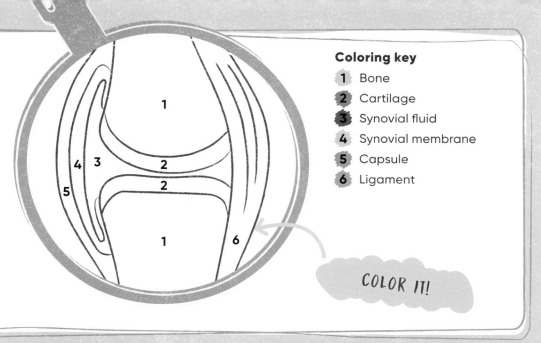

Coloring key

1 Bone
2 Cartilage
3 Synovial fluid
4 Synovial membrane
5 Capsule
6 Ligament

COLOR IT!

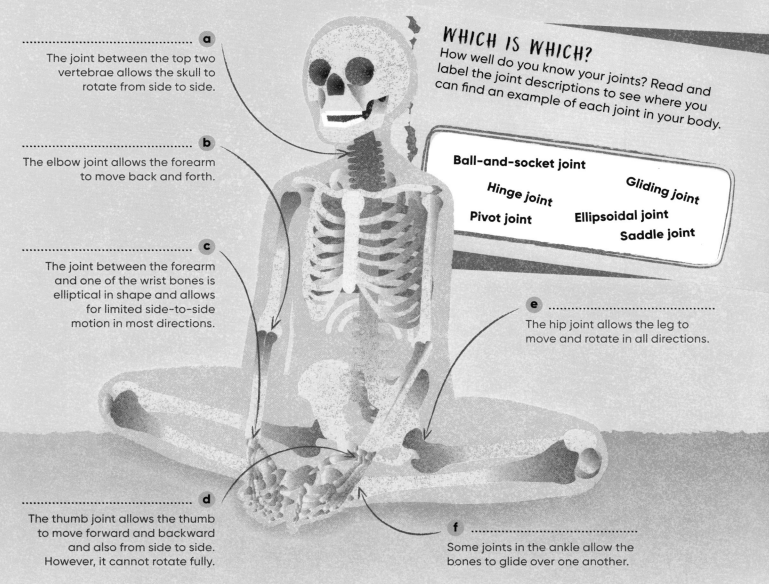

a The joint between the top two vertebrae allows the skull to rotate from side to side.

b The elbow joint allows the forearm to move back and forth.

c The joint between the forearm and one of the wrist bones is elliptical in shape and allows for limited side-to-side motion in most directions.

d The thumb joint allows the thumb to move forward and backward and also from side to side. However, it cannot rotate fully.

WHICH IS WHICH?

How well do you know your joints? Read and label the joint descriptions to see where you can find an example of each joint in your body.

Ball-and-socket joint

Hinge joint   Gliding joint

Pivot joint   Ellipsoidal joint

Saddle joint

e The hip joint allows the leg to move and rotate in all directions.

f Some joints in the ankle allow the bones to glide over one another.

MUSCLE POWER

Muscles are a special type of tissue that contracts (gets smaller) to produce movement. Every time you bend your arm, blow your nose, or take a breath, your muscles are contracting to move the necessary parts of your body.

A lot of muscle

Muscles make up nearly half of your body weight. They help you dance, smile, swallow, and give a thumbs-up. What else do you use your muscles for?

Muscle types

Did you know there are three different types of muscle in your body? Only one type is under your control.

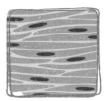

Smooth muscle
Found in the walls of your organs and body parts (such as blood vessels), smooth muscle works without your conscious control.

Cardiac muscle
This forms the walls of your heart and, like smooth muscle, works to pump your heart without you even thinking about it.

Skeletal muscle
This is connected to your bones and helps your body move. These muscles are under your control.

Deltoid
This helps lift the arm to the front, back, and side.

Triceps
It can move your arm down and straightens the elbow.

Extensor digitorum
This extends your fingers.

External oblique
This rotates your body.

Gluteus maximus
It pulls your thigh back to straighten the hip.

Gastrocnemius
It bends your ankle, pulls your heel up, and bends the knee.

Hamstrings
These extend the thigh, bend your knee, and rotate the leg.

Pectoralis major
It pulls your arm in and rotates the shoulder.

Rectus abdominis
This section allows you to bend your body.

Quadriceps
These extend your knee and bend the thigh at the hip.

Tibialis anterior
It bends your foot up toward the shin.

Extensor hallucis longus
This extends your big toe and helps pull your foot up.

WHICH IS WHICH?

Can you tell **smooth** and **cardiac** muscles from **skeletal** ones? Identify each of the three muscle types and then complete the pictures to match the top halves.

WRITE IT!

a ....
Long, even muscle fibers that appear stripy

b ....
Branching muscle fibers that never get tired

c ....
Smaller muscle fibers packed tightly into sheets

FIND THE MISSING MUSCLES

There are more than 640 muscles in the human body, but some are missing here. Color in the missing muscles, using the key below.

Coloring key
- 〰 Triceps
- 〰 Rectus abdominis
- 〰 Quadriceps
- 〰 Gluteus maximus
- 〰 Pectoralis major
- 〰 Hamstrings

COLOR IT!

.... **e**

.... **f**

LABEL IT

Fill in the blank labels, using words from the coloring key.

a ....

b ....

c ....

d ....

WHERE IS THE MUSCLE?

The bulkiest muscle in your body pulls your thigh back to straighten your leg at the hip. It is called the gluteus maximus. Where in your body is the gluteus maximus located? Unscramble the letters to find out.

O N T Y M B O R O U

_ _   _ _ _ _ _
_ _ _ _ _

FLEXING YOUR MUSCLES

Muscles contract (get smaller) to pull bones toward each other and move the body. This is known as flexing. But muscles cannot push—they can only relax once the pulling is done. That's why most muscles work in pairs. One pulls the bone one way, and then the other pulls it back.

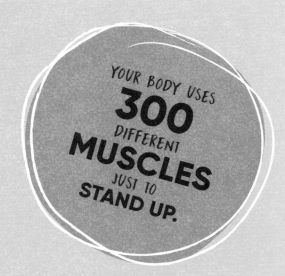

YOUR BODY USES **300** DIFFERENT **MUSCLES** JUST TO **STAND UP.**

LABEL THE MUSCLES

Every tiny facial expression you make is controlled by muscles. Read these cards and then label each muscle correctly.

Orbicularis oris
This band of muscles brings your lips together and helps you form sounds.

Masseter
This muscle helps you chew by moving your jaw.

Zygomaticus major
This muscle pulls the corner of your mouth up and out, allowing you to smile.

Orbicularis oculi
This ring of muscles around your eye helps close your eyelid.

Temporalis
These chewing muscles are attached to the side of your forehead.

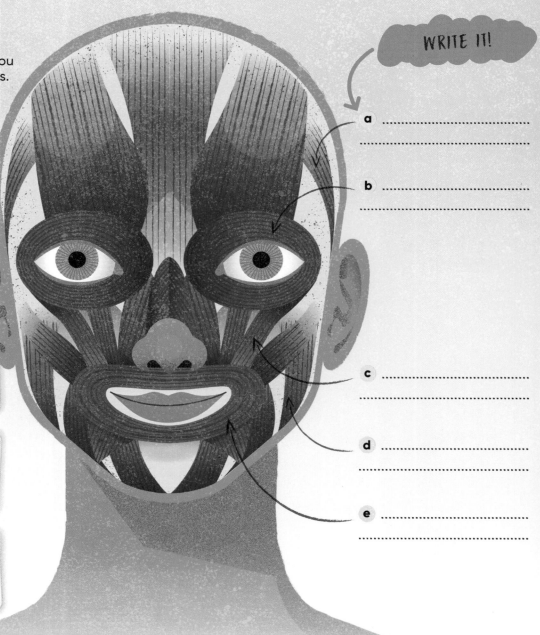

WRITE IT!

a ....
....

b ....
....

c ....
....

d ....
....

e ....
....

14

Muscle pairs

A pair of muscles work together to move a part of the body one way and then back again. The biceps and triceps are a well-known muscle pair—maybe it's because their names rhyme!

BICEPS

TRICEPS

Flex that biceps
When the biceps contracts, it pulls the bones in the lower arm toward the upper arm, bending the elbow. The triceps is relaxed.

BICEPS

TRICEPS

Flex that triceps
To straighten your elbow, the biceps relaxes while the triceps contracts, pulling the bones in the lower arm down.

Biceps
This muscle is at the front of your upper arm.

Triceps
This muscle is at the back of your upper arm.

FLEXING OR RESTING?

Color in the muscles that are flexing and resting on these diagrams. Use red for contracting muscles and blue for relaxing muscles.

Coloring key

〰 Contracting

〰 Relaxing

COLOR IT!

Quadriceps
This group of muscles is at the front of your thigh.

Hamstrings
This group of muscles is at the back of your thigh.

WORK IT OUT!

Your muscles are attached to your bones with hard, strong cords called tendons. The body's strongest tendon is the Achilles tendon. Solve the equation below to find out how many times your body weight it can carry.

Achilles tendon

(84 − 28) ÷ 8 = ?

....

THE NERVOUS SYSTEM

Inside the body is a network of nerve cells that carries speedy electrical signals around the body, including to and from the brain. This system controls everything about you, from breathing and blinking to how you think. Millions of these lightning-fast signals are sent every day.

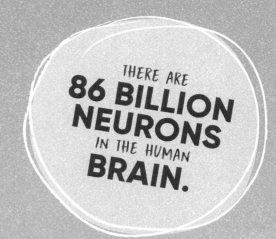

THERE ARE **86 BILLION NEURONS** IN THE HUMAN **BRAIN.**

Nerve map

Nerves branch out from the brain and spinal cord to reach all parts of your body. There are 12 pairs of nerves from the brain and 31 pairs from the spinal cord.

Brain
The brain controls the nervous system, processing incoming signals and sending new signals out.

Spinal cord
Together, the spinal cord and brain make up the central nervous system.

Nerves
Nerves that branch out from the brain and spinal cord make up the peripheral nervous system.

WORK OUT THE STAGES

The brain receives signals from the nervous system and sends signals to the body. These five steps show how your body reacts when you pick up an object, such as an apple. Fill in the numbers for each step on the diagram below.

1 Sense receptors in your hand feel that you're holding something.

2 The nerve network passes a signal along until it reaches the spinal cord.

3 The spinal cord sends the signal to the brain, where it is processed.

4 The brain sends another signal down the spinal cord to the bicep muscle.

5 The bicep muscle contracts, allowing your hand to lift the apple to your mouth.

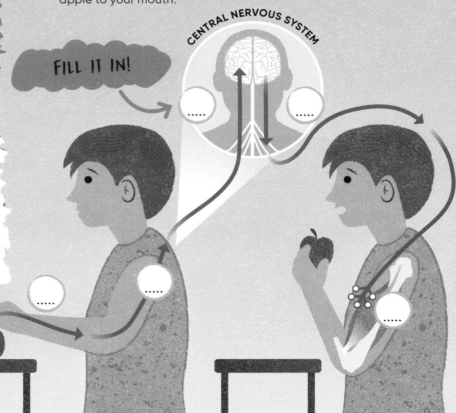

CENTRAL NERVOUS SYSTEM

FILL IT IN!

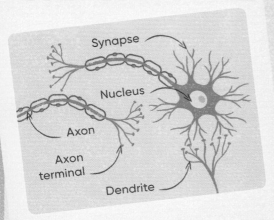

Synapse

Nucleus

Axon

Axon terminal

Dendrite

Neurons

Nerve cells, or neurons, receive and send nerve signals. The cells usually have a long body and spiky fibers at each end. The place where two neurons meet is called a synapse.

FOLLOW THE SIGNALS

A neuron receives a signal via the dendrites. The signal flows along the axon and is passed to the next neuron at the axon terminal. Draw the path of each signal as it makes its way through the neurons to the spinal cord and brain.

START HERE

FINISH HERE

START HERE

START HERE

MATCH THE MOVEMENTS

Sometimes we can control our body's actions, but some actions happen automatically—these are known as reflexes. Can you match these reflexes to the correct image?

MATCH IT!

a

b

c

d

Blink
Your eyelids blink if anything comes close to or touches your eyes.

Gag
To prevent choking, your throat contracts when something touches too far inside your mouth.

Knee-jerk
Doctors test your reflexes by tapping a point on your knee to see if your leg jerks.

Pupils dilate
Your pupils react to changes in light. They grow larger when it's dark to help you see better.

THE BRAIN

Protected inside the skull is your body's control center. The brain coordinates almost every action and movement that you perform and is responsible for every thought or feeling that you have. It has three main parts—the largest is the cerebrum, below that is the cerebellum, and the brain stem links your brain to your spinal cord.

UNSCRAMBLE IT!
Can you find a lobe of the brain hidden in this word scramble?

P R
A O I T
L E A E B
E L

_ _ _ _ _ _ _

_ _ _ _

Brain anatomy

The cerebrum is divided into two halves (left and right), and each side has four lobes. Together, they allow you to do such things as see, hear, speak, and learn. The cerebellum coordinates posture and balance. And the brain stem controls automatic functions, such as heart rate and breathing.

Parietal lobe
This interprets signals from your senses, such as touch, smell, vision, and muscle movements.

Occipital lobe
This is the main area for your vision—processing color, light, and motion.

Cerebellum
Combined with information from your senses, this coordinates movement.

Brain stem
This manages basic bodily functions and links the brain to the body.

Frontal lobe
This is responsible for such things as your personality, learning, problem solving, speaking, and writing.

Temporal lobe
This contains areas for memory, hearing, organizing things, and understanding language.

MAKE THE CONNECTION

The nerve cells (neurons) that make up the brain connect with each other in a complicated network. Read the descriptions and use the word box to label three parts of the connected network inside the brain.

Gray matter   White matter
Corpus callosum

a
Tightly packed nerve-cell bodies form an outer, gray area of the cerebrum.

b
Long fibers (axons) from the nerve-cell bodies form an inner, white area of the brain.

c
This curved area is where bundles of nerve fibers carry information from one side of the brain to the other.

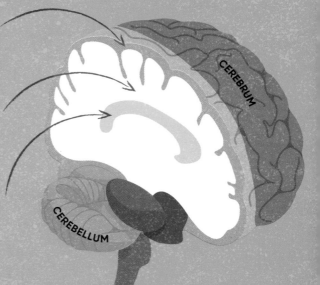

CEREBRUM

CEREBELLUM

18

THE **RIGHT** SIDE OF THE BRAIN **CONTROLS THE LEFT** SIDE OF THE BODY (AND VICE VERSA)!

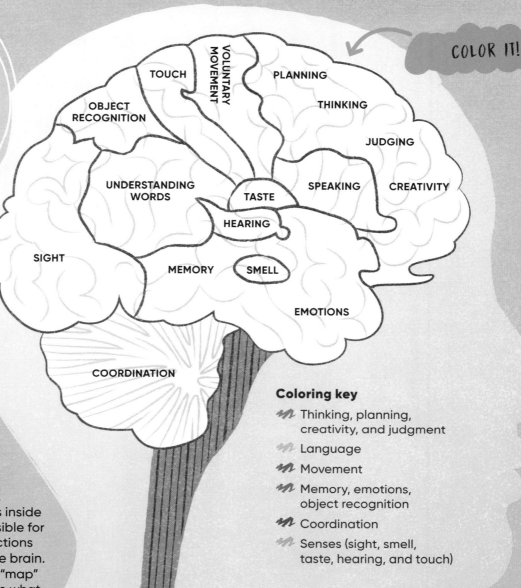

TOUCH

VOLUNTARY MOVEMENT

OBJECT RECOGNITION

PLANNING

THINKING

JUDGING

UNDERSTANDING WORDS

TASTE

SPEAKING

CREATIVITY

HEARING

SIGHT

MEMORY

SMELL

EMOTIONS

COORDINATION

Coloring key

〰 Thinking, planning, creativity, and judgment

〰 Language

〰 Movement

〰 Memory, emotions, object recognition

〰 Coordination

〰 Senses (sight, smell, taste, hearing, and touch)

THINK ABOUT THIS!

There are smaller sections inside the brain that are responsible for different actions. Some actions involve several parts of the brain. Use the key to color in this "map" of the brain, so you can see what happens where.

WHICH IS WHICH?

Scientists use scans to map the brain and learn more about how it works. Here are three different types of brain scans—can you match them to their descriptions below?

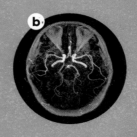

a.

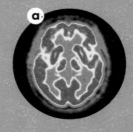

b.

c.

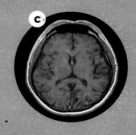

MATCH IT!

MRA
Uses a magnetic field and radio waves to create an intricate black-and-white image of the brain's blood vessels

MRI
Also uses a magnetic field and radio waves to create a black-and-white image of the folded structure of the cerebrum and cerebellum

PET
Creates a colorful 3D image of the brain that can show how well different areas are working

TONGUE

THE VOICE

When you speak, you're using the air itself to make sound. Your voice is the sound your vocal cords make as air from your lungs pushes past them. The changing vibrations of the cords are what make different sounds.

Forming words
Your breath carries the sounds of your voice to your mouth, where you transform the sounds into words. Your lips, cheeks, tongue, and teeth can all control the flow of air to help make specific sounds.

Epiglottis
This small flap of tissue blocks the entrance to the larynx when you eat.

Vocal cords
These small bands of muscle and tissue open and close inside the larynx.

Larynx
This short tube connects the throat to the trachea.

Trachea
Air travels to and from your lungs through this windpipe.

WRITE IT!

FIND YOUR VOICE
We use our voice to communicate in different ways. What do you use your voice for? Unscramble these words to reveal four ways you can use your voice.

H U T I S O G N

N I G S I G N

a ....

b ....

T G T C H I A N

A I G G U N L H

c ....

d ....

FIND THE WORDS

There are many small parts of the body that help us speak. See if you can find them all in the wordsearch.

```
        S B N A L
    O R O X G T Y O E M
  G R I P Q T C Y N F A C O
 G E I V O C A L C O R D S B H
E S A C D A Y F U P T Y N Y R E
I R T S A G F R B U O H K R E J
L I P H P I U M K M O N E F D O
G E F T H V S E E P I G L O T X
N N O U I O M O E D N U O D N H
 Z F O N T D V C F A E V I P T
 R P M V M S A X N Y R A L A B
  R O T M E H G Q I J D V E I
    R P R G U N T R A C H E
      R C F T A O L B X
        Q E N A T P
```

Epiglottis **Larynx**
Trachea **Tongue** **Breath**
Vocal cords **Mouth**

WHAT ARE YOU SAYING?

Can you identify the mouth shape needed to make these sounds? Draw a line between the pictures and the matching sounds.

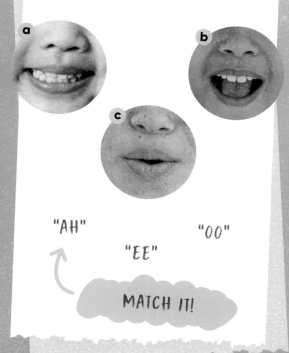

a
b
c

"AH"   "OO"
    "EE"

MATCH IT!

WHICH IS WHICH?

Your vocal cords stretch across the larynx. When you are not talking, they relax, allowing your breath to flow in and out. When you speak, they close across the tube, leaving just a small gap. As air goes through the gap, the cords vibrate to make a sound.

1. Label the two diagrams, using the word pool above.

2. Then, use the coloring key to color the arrows in the diagrams on the right to show which one is breath and which one is voice.

Breathing
Speaking

Coloring key
〰 Voice
〰 Breath

COLOR IT!

OPEN VOCAL CORDS

CLOSED VOCAL CORDS

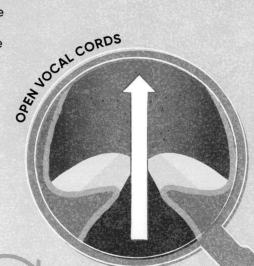

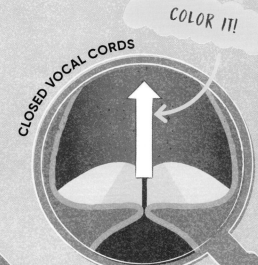

WRITE IT!

a ....

b ....

21

SENSES

There's so much going on around you, and it's your senses that transmit all that information to your brain. Different senses receive different information—a feeling of cold, a bright light, or the smell of a flower—and your brain puts it all together.

TOUCH
Touch receptor cells in the skin sense temperature, pain, pressure, and vibration.

HEARING
Your ear turns sound waves into nerve signals so that the brain can interpret them.

SIGHT
Light waves enter your eyes and are turned into signals that tell your brain what you see.

Motor cortex

Somatosensory cortex

Primary taste area

Auditory cortex

Visual cortex

Olfactory cortex

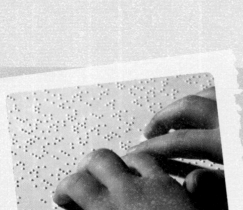

Working together
When a person loses one of their senses, the other senses become stronger in order to help make up for the loss. For example, blind people can learn to read Braille by using their sense of touch.

Six senses
We think of humans as having five senses: touch, hearing, sight, taste, and smell. But there is a sixth sense called proprioception. Each sense gathers information and sends it to a different part of the brain to be processed.

MAKE SENSE OF THE WORLD
Everything you know about the world is thanks to your senses. Your brain builds a multilayered view of what you see, hear, smell, taste, and feel and where you are in all of it. Can you draw a picture to show each sense in action?

DRAW IT!

Feel it!

Breathe it in

PROPRIOCEPTION

Receptors in your joints and muscles let your brain know where each part of your body is and how it is moving.

TASTE

Taste receptor cells in the tongue identify different flavors and help us know which foods are safe to eat.

SMELL

When you breathe in or sniff, scent particles enter your nose. The brain can tell the difference between billions of smells.

COMPLETE IT!

DON'T THINK ABOUT IT

Proprioception is your sixth sense. It helps you carry out actions without having to consciously plan each muscle movement. Can you think of three activities that use this sense?

a ....

b ....

c ....

REVEAL THE WORD

What do we have all over our body that help us sense what's going on around us? Cross out the letters of the word "sensory" to reveal the answer!

R S E E C N E P S T O R O R Y S

_ _ _ _ _ _ _ _ _

What a view!

Can you hear it?

Full of flavor

Keep on moving

TOUCHY-FEELY

Your sense of touch comes from sensory receptors in your skin. These are specialized nerve endings that can sense heat, cold, pressure, and pain. When the receptor senses something, it sends a signal along the nerve to the brain for processing.

Sensory receptors

Different sensory receptors can be found in the different layers of the skin. They are all specialized to measure changes in touch, such as light or heavy pressure or low, medium, or intense heat. Here are some of the main types of receptor.

THERE ARE UP TO 3,000 RECEPTORS ON EACH FINGERTIP!

Epidermis
This top layer of skin provides a waterproof barrier and gives your skin its color.

Dermis
This thick layer of skin is made of tough tissue and contains most of your sensory receptors.

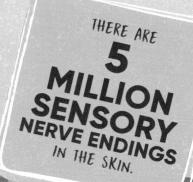

THERE ARE
5 MILLION SENSORY NERVE ENDINGS IN THE SKIN.

Ruffini corpuscle
These detect joint movement, so they help you grip objects. They also detect warmth.

Meissner's corpuscle
Sensing light touch and vibrations, these are plentiful in your eyelids.

Merkel's disc
There are lots of these receptors in your fingertips and lips because they sense fine details.

Free nerve endings
These are the most abundant receptors, sensing pain and injury.

Pacinian corpuscle
These large nerve endings, located deeper in the dermis, detect hard pressure.

MAKE SENSE OF IT!

Can you tell which of these three sensory receptors would sense each type of stimulus below? Hint: The illustration and labels on the left will help you.

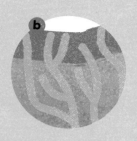

a

b

c

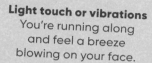

MATCH IT!

Pain or injury
You're walking along the beach and accidentally stub your toe on a big rock.

Light touch or vibrations
You're running along and feel a breeze blowing on your face.

Fine details and texture
It's dark, and you reach over to find the switch for your bedside lamp.

DRAW YOURSELF

A sensory homunculus is a figure showing exaggerated features for areas of the human body that have the most sensory receptors. The word homunculus means "little man" in Latin. Draw a sensory homunculus, like the Little Blue Man to the right, to represent your own body.

Little Blue Man
Some of the most sensitive areas of your body are your hands, feet, lips, and tongue, as shown in our Little Blue Man, above.

Lips and tongue
These are very sensitive to touch. They help you understand what you are eating or drinking.

DRAW IT!

Hands and fingertips
These are extremely touch-sensitive because we explore and identify things with our hands.

Feet
These sense the ground you are on. They may also be very ticklish because they are so sensitive.

Inside the eye

When light enters the eye, it is focused onto the retina at the back of the eyeball. The retina turns this image into nerve signals, which are sent to the brain.

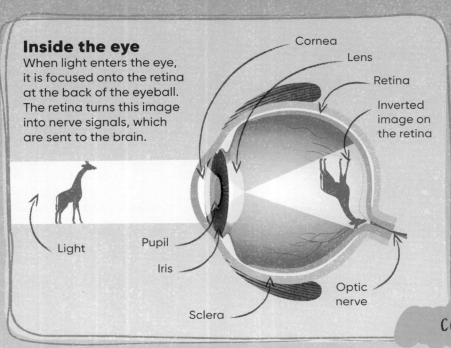

Cornea
Lens
Retina
Inverted image on the retina
Light
Pupil
Iris
Optic nerve
Sclera

FILL IN THE BLANKS

Use the information on the left to help you fill in the correct names for each part of the eye. There are some clues in the descriptions to help you out.

.... **a**
A transparent disk that helps adjust vision for near or far objects

COLOR IT!

FLIP THE CAT

Because the eye is curved, light bends as it travels through the cornea. This means that the image created on the retina is upside down. Draw how this cat will appear at the back of the large eye (right).

INSPECT YOUR IRIS

Find a mirror and take a close look at your irises. Color the iris on this diagram to match your own.

THE EYE

Our eyes are like amazing machines, with lots of different parts working together. When we look at something, light rays bounce off it and enter our eyes, giving us information about its shape and color. Almost instantly, the eye processes these light rays and turns them into signals the brain can understand.

.... **b**
Your eye's clear, outer layer

.... **c**
A hole in the eye through which light rays can enter

.... **d**
A ring of muscles around the pupil that control its size

.... **e**
The white, protective outer layer of the eyeball

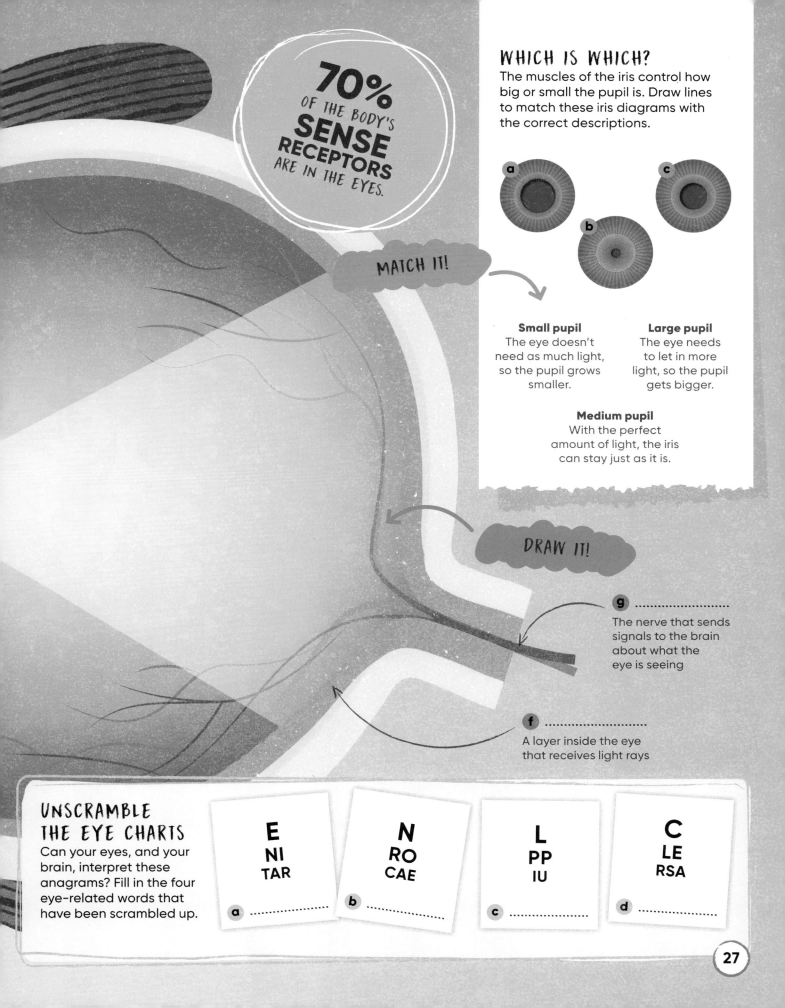

WHICH IS WHICH?

The muscles of the iris control how big or small the pupil is. Draw lines to match these iris diagrams with the correct descriptions.

a

c

b

MATCH IT!

Small pupil
The eye doesn't need as much light, so the pupil grows smaller.

Large pupil
The eye needs to let in more light, so the pupil gets bigger.

Medium pupil
With the perfect amount of light, the iris can stay just as it is.

70% OF THE BODY'S SENSE RECEPTORS ARE IN THE EYES.

DRAW IT!

g ....
The nerve that sends signals to the brain about what the eye is seeing

f ....
A layer inside the eye that receives light rays

UNSCRAMBLE THE EYE CHARTS

Can your eyes, and your brain, interpret these anagrams? Fill in the four eye-related words that have been scrambled up.

E NI TAR

a ....

N RO CAE

b ....

L PP IU

c ....

C LE RSA

d ....

SEEING THINGS

What you see makes up more than half of the information your brain receives. That's a lot! Vision is obviously important to us. However, it isn't always perfect. Some people wear glasses or contact lenses to correct their vision. The brain may also become confused when it tries to interpret certain images that it receives from the eye.

ONLY **35%** OF PEOPLE HAVE **PERFECT VISION.**

Visual cortex
The brain interprets information from the eye inside the visual cortex. It doesn't just process what we see but actively tries to make sense of it. That's why there is room for confusion—it's possible to trick the brain!

Visual data travel along the optic nerve to the visual cortex.

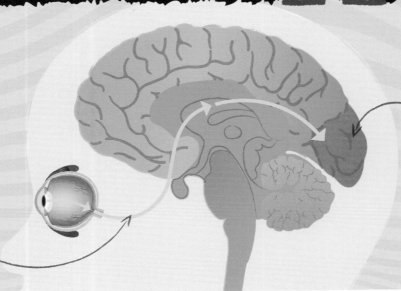

The visual cortex sorts the data by shape, color, location, and movement. The brain then searches your memory for similar visual information.

WHAT DO YOU SEE?
Our brains use past experiences and logic to understand what we see, but this can lead to errors. Optical illusions are specifically created to fool the brain into seeing things differently than how they really are. Check what you see!

CHECK IT!

a Are the vertical lines parallel or bending away from each other?

☐ Parallel
☐ Bending away
☐ Neither

b Which red line is longer?

☐ Top
☐ Bottom
☐ They are the same

c What do you see?

☐ A vase
☐ Two faces
☐ Both

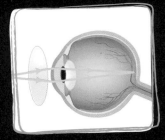

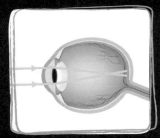

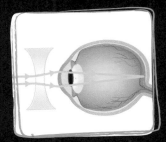

Farsighted eye
The eyeball is too short, so the image of what we see is focused beyond the retina. This makes objects near the person look blurry.

Convex lens
A convex lens corrects farsightedness by helping the rays of light come together so they meet on the retina.

Nearsighted eye
The eyeball is too long, so the image of what we see is focused in front of the retina. This makes objects far away look blurry.

Concave lens
A concave lens corrects nearsightedness by helping the rays of light split apart so they meet on the retina.

WHICH LENS?

These images show how farsighted vision differs from nearsighted vision. Which type of lenses would be needed in a pair of glasses to correct vision for each one? Circle the lens shape required under each picture.

CIRCLE IT!

a Convex / Concave

b Convex / Concave

FIND THE NUMBERS

Can you see any numbers in these circles? People who are color-blind cannot differentiate between certain colors, or they might only see gray dots. Draw over the numbers (if you can see them!) and write what they are below.

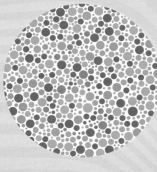

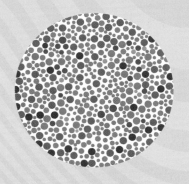

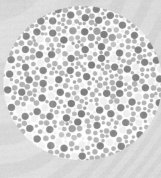

a ....

b ....

c ....

Inside the ear

There are three parts to the ear: the outer, middle, and inner ear. Sound waves travel into the outer ear and through the canal to the middle ear, where they are amplified. The inner ear fluids then convert the wave vibrations into nerve signals.

Semicircular canals
This is the part of the inner ear system that controls balance.

Cochlea
A fluid-filled organ in the inner ear that converts vibrations into nerve signals

Ossicles
These three tiny bones in the middle ear pass the vibrations along to the cochlea.

Vestibulocochlear nerve
This nerve transmits signals to the brain.

Eustachian tube
This leads to the throat and helps regulate middle ear pressure.

Ear canal
This channels sound waves into the ear.

Eardrum
A thin membrane of skin that vibrates from sound waves

Outer ear
It is trumpet-shaped to funnel sound waves inside.

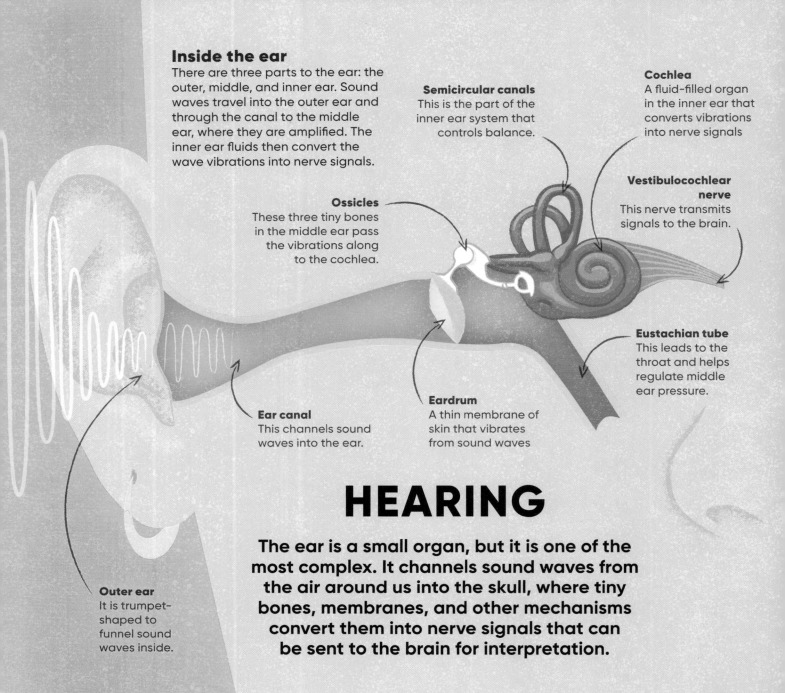

HEARING

The ear is a small organ, but it is one of the most complex. It channels sound waves from the air around us into the skull, where tiny bones, membranes, and other mechanisms convert them into nerve signals that can be sent to the brain for interpretation.

HOW LOUD?

We measure sounds on the decibel scale. The louder the sound, the higher the number of decibels. Add the missing sounds below to the labels in order of how loud you think they are and then draw a picture for all six sounds measured.

Space shuttle blast-off
Leaves rustling
City traffic

DECIBELS

0	20	40	60	80

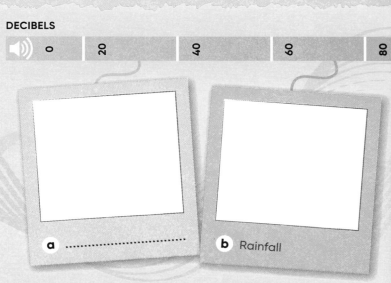

a ....

b Rainfall

COLOR ME IN

Use the key to color in this diagram of the ear. See if you can remember which part is which—or refer to the diagram on the left if you get stuck!

Coloring key
- Eardrum
- Ossicles
- Cochlea
- Vestibulocochlear nerve
- Eustachian tube
- Semicircular canals
- Ear canal

YOUR EARS ARE WORKING EVEN WHEN YOU **SLEEP!**

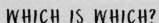

COLOR IT!

WHICH IS WHICH?

Sound waves make a complex pattern of vibrations, which travel through the air and into our ears. Can you match the different parts of the ear (shown in pink) to the descriptions below?

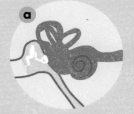

a

b

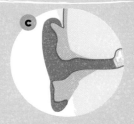

c

Middle ear
A sound chamber where the eardrum and ossicles amplify the vibrations

Outer ear
The external part of the ear that receives sound waves from the air around you

Inner ear
A fluid-filled system that uses tiny hairs to convert the vibrations into nerve signals

MATCH IT!

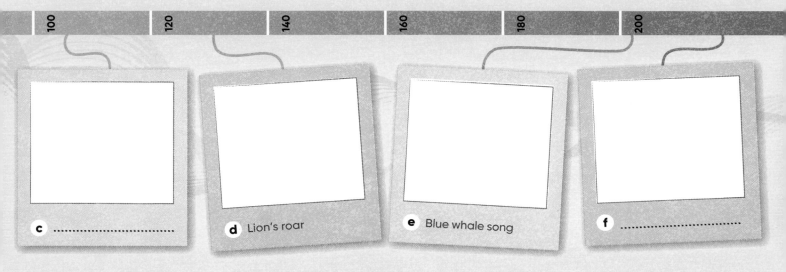

100 120 140 160 180 200

c ....

d Lion's roar

e Blue whale song

f ....

SMELL

From cooking aromas and sweet fragrances to bad odors, our noses can tell the difference between 1 trillion smells! This is thanks to the tiny receptor cells in our noses that pick up different chemicals in the food we eat and the air we breathe in and send them to the brain for processing.

Receptor cells

Scent molecules float into your nose and reach your receptor cells, which send nerve impulses to the olfactory bulb. The brain then decides how you should react—by running, for example, if it's a fire.

Supporting cell

Olfactory receptor cell

Mucus-secreting gland

Mucus

Scent molecule

Olfactory bulb
This brain tissue receives information about smell and sends it farther into the brain for more processing.

Nasal cavity
This is where scent molecules are detected inside your nose.

Nose hair
Hair and mucus inside the nostrils trap most dirt and germs in the air.

NASAL CAVITY

TONGUE

Food aromas
Scent molecules from food in the mouth also enter the nasal cavity.

Scents in the air
Tiny scent molecules float into your nasal cavity and dissolve in mucus.

HUMANS CAN TELL THE DIFFERENCE BETWEEN 1 TRILLION SMELLS!

WHAT'S THAT SMELL?

There are ten basic types of smells, which range from the pungent smell of stinky cheese to the chemical smell of bleach. Draw something in each of the circles on the right that smells lemony, sweet, and minty.

NUTTY

CHEMICAL

WOODY

PUNGENT

FRAGRANT

DECAYED

DRAW IT!

SWEET

MINTY

FRUITY

LEMONY

FIND THE WORDS

The parts of your body that deal with smell make up the olfactory system. Can you find the smell-related words in the wordsearch below?

Cavity	Mucus	Nose
	Olfactory	Scent
Receptor		

FIND IT!

```
                    H Y Q U U O P
      F J N R U B G L Q V B G C R I J K
        Y C O L F A C T O R Y W C H A S X C I
A T N A C S V Z D H L P T O A I N S Z D I C T R D J O
B Z W O Y I C Y N X H A E S E V O T Y E E I U E E E P
C F I L P L A G I A S U I A P S B I X Z N K M U C U S Q
              T S S E J T T I P Y W E G O R
                O Y T U Z R P H N S
                  I U A E D T I P T
                  P F S Y O B N M
                  W R T R U O P
                  B E I M H Y
                  A S D F G J
                  T P L B Z
                  U J E B
```

CRACK THE NOSE CODE

Having a cold or hay fever can lead to a loss of smell. To find the word for losing your sense of smell, replace each of the letters in this nose with the letter before it in the alphabet. Hint: zigzag down from the top.

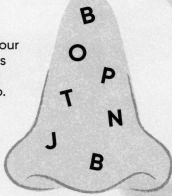

_ _ _ _ _ _ _ _

The tongue

When you eat, your strong, muscular tongue moves the food around in your mouth. It is covered in tiny, sensitive bumps called papillae and is connected to the brain by nerves.

80% OF THE **FLAVOR** WE DETECT IN FOOD COMES FROM OUR **SENSE OF SMELL.**

Circumvallate papillae
These are located near the back of the tongue and contain taste buds.

Foliate papillae
They run down the sides on the back part of the tongue. These papillae contain several hundred taste buds.

Filiform papillae
These papillae cover most of the tongue. They don't contain taste buds.

Fungiform papillae
These are mostly on the tip and sides of the tongue and contain taste buds.

TASTE

When you eat something, your tongue helps you identify the taste. Thousands of taste buds line your tongue, and they let your brain know whether your food is bitter, sweet, salty, sour, umami (savory), or a combination of these. Our sense of smell works with our taste buds to allow us to identify hundreds of thousands of different flavors in our food and drink.

FIND THE WORDS
Find these tongue-tastic words in the word search below.

```
T E E H K B F X V N
G B I T T E R I O F W
F Y A C R G T V H P P Q
I R Y T L A R E E K A U
D T Y S O X G J K N P J
M E N V P N I U A B I M
X E Y J D A G O F N L R
U W N H R M D U O P L K
Q S A L T Y P M E U A T
F W R A U L D A O P E F
S D H P H U V M N R N I
Z J I E A F I I L I H J
V R U O S B O U G X E E
```

Tongue   Sweet
Salty   Sour   Bitter
Papillae   Umami

COLOR THE TASTE BUD

A child has about 10,000 taste buds! Each one contains receptor cells that send nerve signals to your brain, telling it what the food tastes like. Color in this taste bud, using the coloring key below.

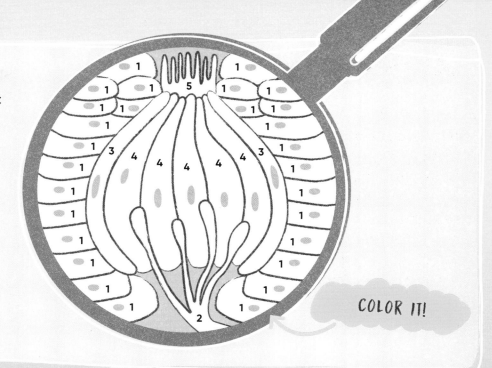

Coloring key

1. Tongue skin cell
2. Nerve fiber
3. Supporting cell
4. Taste receptor cell
5. Taste hairs

COLOR IT!

REVEAL THE SUPERTASTER

Did you know, some people have more taste buds than others? These "supertasters" can taste things others can't. Which of the tongues below belongs to the **normal taster**, and which belongs to the **supertaster**? Write the correct answer under each.

SUPERTASTERS MAKE UP **25%** OF THE POPULATION.

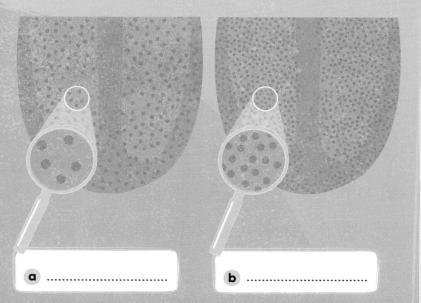

a ....

b ....

SOLVE THE TASTE-OKU

Complete the sudoku grid below. Each section, row, and column must contain all five tastes.

Key

- Lemon (sour)
- Coffee (bitter)
- Salt (salty)
- Mushroom (umami)
- Ice cream (sweet)

BREATHING

Take a deep breath. You've just expanded your lungs like a pair of balloons, pulling air into your body. Lungs are our breathing machines. They take oxygen out of the air and into our bloodstreams, and they remove carbon dioxide waste from the blood, which we breathe back out.

How the lungs work

Every breath you take goes down into your lungs, where it flows through thousands of many-branching tubes called bronchi. The bronchi grow smaller and smaller until they end at tiny air sacs —known as alveoli—where oxygen can enter the bloodstream.

IN OR OUT?

When you breathe, your diaphragm moves up and down. Label the illustrations below with either **breathing in** or **breathing out**. Hint: The blue arrows show the direction of the air inside the lungs, and the red arrows show the movement of the chest.

a ....   b ....

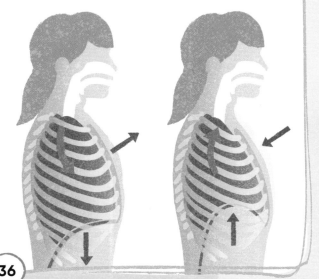

CILIA

Tiny hairlike cilia line the trachea, catching any dirt and germs in the air.

Trachea
Your windpipe carries air to and from the lungs.

Bronchi
These are branches of the lungs' airways that get smaller and smaller.

Heart
This side of the heart pumps blood to the lungs.

Protective membranes
Soft tissue covers each lung to protect it.

Ribs
Your lungs and heart are protected inside this bone "cage."

ALVEOLI

Millions of tiny sacs surrounded by blood vessels give a huge surface area for oxygen and carbon dioxide to pass between the lungs and the bloodstream.

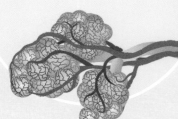

Diaphragm
This large muscle controls your breathing by expanding the chest cavity when you breathe in.

FINISH THE PICTURE
Your lungs and heart work together to supply your body with oxygen. Use the key below to color in the illustration.

Coloring key

∿ Trachea
∿ Ribs
∿ Bronchi
∿ Heart
∿ Protective membrane
∿ Diaphragm

COLOR IT!

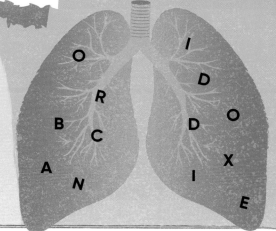

YOUR LUNGS CONTAIN **MORE THAN 300 MILLION ALVEOLI.**

UNSCRAMBLE IT
Not only do our lungs take in oxygen, but they also get rid of another gas, which is released by our cells when they create energy. Unscramble the letters in each lung to reveal the name of that gas.

O R B C A N
I D D O X I E

WRITE IT!

_ _ _ _ _ _   _ _ _ _ _ _

HOW MANY BREATHS?
Did you know that the older you are, the slower you breathe? Match these timers showing breaths per minute to the correct ages.

MATCH IT!

a   **b**   **c**

1–3 years old
The lungs are small, so young children take 24–40 breaths per minute.

6–12 years old
Lung capacity increases, so children only need 18–30 breaths per minute.

Over 18 years old
Adult lung capacity means that only 12–20 breaths are needed per minute.

WE BREATHE IN AROUND **2,900 GALLONS** (11,000 LITERS) OF AIR A DAY!

THE CIRCULATORY SYSTEM

The circulatory system is made up of your heart and blood vessels. Your heart pumps blood through a network of tubes called blood vessels. Blood vessels carry blood to each cell in your body to deliver essentials for life and to collect waste products.

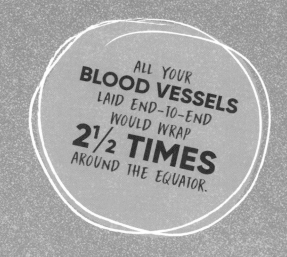

ALL YOUR **BLOOD VESSELS** LAID END-TO-END WOULD WRAP **2½ TIMES** AROUND THE EQUATOR.

Blood vessels

There are three types of blood vessels in your body: arteries, veins, and the tiny capillaries that infuse your tissues with blood and link your arteries and veins.

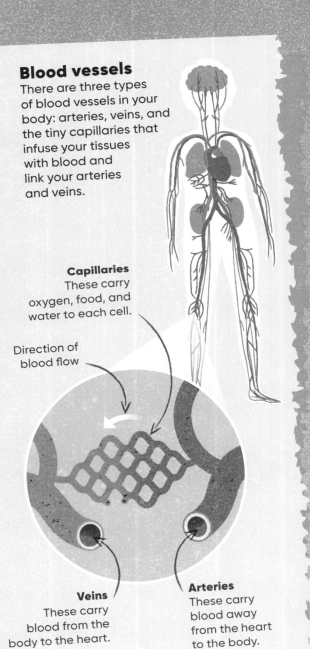

Capillaries
These carry oxygen, food, and water to each cell.

Direction of blood flow

Veins
These carry blood from the body to the heart.

Arteries
These carry blood away from the heart to the body.

FILL IN THE OXYGEN LOOPS

Our circulatory system is made up of two "loops." One loop pumps blood from the heart to the lungs to pick up oxygen, and the other loop pumps oxygen-rich blood from the heart around your body. Use the key to color in the two loops, then finish the sentences with either **body** or **lungs**.

Coloring key

1 Blood rich in oxygen
2 Blood poor in oxygen

COLOR IT!

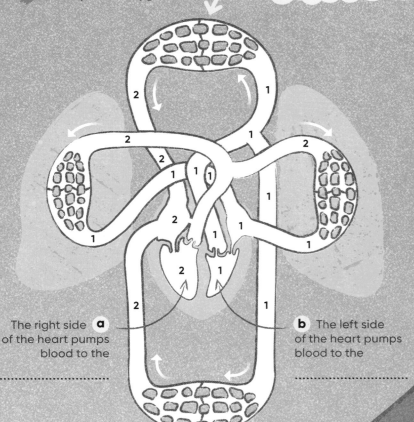

The right side **a** of the heart pumps blood to the
....

b The left side of the heart pumps blood to the
....

38

MATCH THE BLOOD VESSELS

Read the descriptions below and draw a line to the blood vessel that matches it.

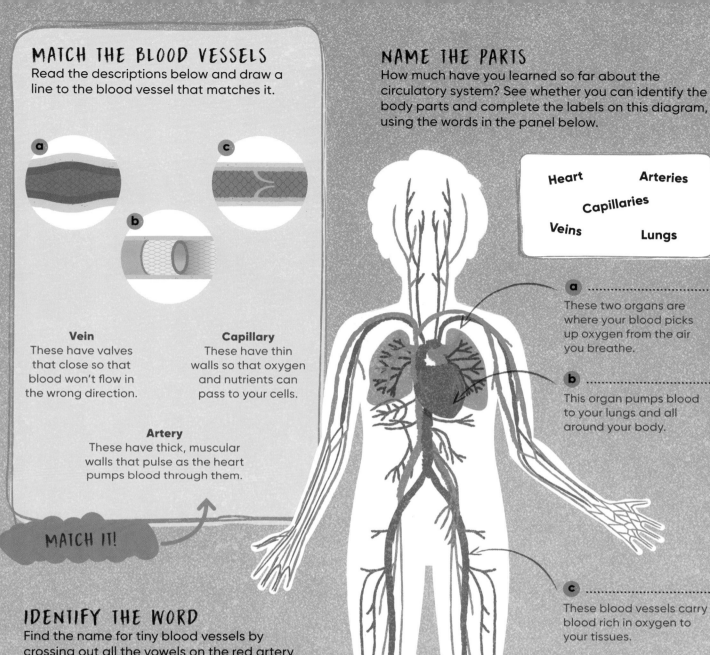

Vein
These have valves that close so that blood won't flow in the wrong direction.

Capillary
These have thin walls so that oxygen and nutrients can pass to your cells.

Artery
These have thick, muscular walls that pulse as the heart pumps blood through them.

MATCH IT!

NAME THE PARTS

How much have you learned so far about the circulatory system? See whether you can identify the body parts and complete the labels on this diagram, using the words in the panel below.

Heart   Arteries

Capillaries

Veins   Lungs

a ....
These two organs are where your blood picks up oxygen from the air you breathe.

b ....
This organ pumps blood to your lungs and all around your body.

c ....
These blood vessels carry blood rich in oxygen to your tissues.

d ....
These blood vessels carry blood low in oxygen back to your heart.

e ....
These tiny blood vessels supply blood to each cell and connect the small veins and arteries.

IDENTIFY THE WORD

Find the name for tiny blood vessels by crossing out all the vowels on the red artery and all the consonants on the blue vein. Rearrange the leftover letters to find your answer.

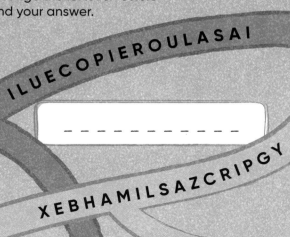

ILUECOPIEROULASAI

XEBHAMILSAZCRIPGY

_ _ _ _ _ _ _ _ _ _

39

In and out
Your heart works continuously, pumping blood to and from your lungs and body. The right side receives blood low in oxygen and pumps it to your lungs. The left side receives blood high in oxygen and pumps it all over your body.

Superior vena cava
This large vein returns blood from your head and upper body to your heart.

Right atrium
Blood low in oxygen flows into here from around your body.

Heart wall
This is made of a special kind of muscle that never gets tired.

Valve
This ensures blood flows only one way. There are four valves in the heart.

Right ventricle
This chamber has strong muscles to squeeze blood through the valve to your lungs.

Inferior vena cava
Your largest vein, this returns blood to the heart from your lower body.

Aorta
The largest artery in your body, this carries blood from the heart to your body.

Pulmonary artery
Taking blood to your lungs, it is the only artery in your body that carries blood low in oxygen.

Pulmonary vein
This brings blood full of oxygen back from your lungs to your heart.

Left atrium
Oxygen-rich blood flows into here from your lungs.

Left ventricle
This has strong muscles that squeeze blood through the valve to your aorta.

THE HEART

Your heart sits inside your chest, in between your lungs and slightly to the left side. It is a muscular organ with four chambers (two atria and two ventricles) that pump blood around your body. If you put your hand on your chest, you can feel the chambers squeezing and relaxing—this is your heartbeat.

YOUR HEART WILL BEAT MORE THAN **2.5 BILLION** TIMES BY THE TIME YOU ARE **70 YEARS OLD.**

DECIPHER THE HEART PARTS

Unscramble each word in the red blood cells. Then, label the heart below with the correct letter.

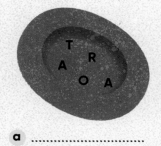

a ....

b ....

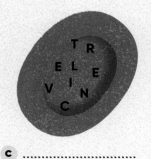

c ....

d ....

e ....

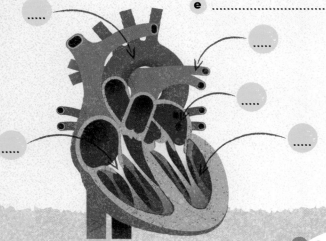

FIND YOUR PULSE

As each heartbeat forces blood through your arteries, they bulge—this is called your pulse. A doctor or nurse uses an electrocardiogram (ECG) to check the heart's rhythm, or pulse. Connect the dots below. One pulse is **regular** and one is **irregular**. Write which one is which beside each patient.

PATIENT A: ....

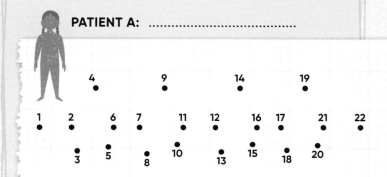

PATIENT B: ....

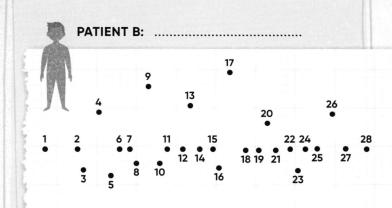

WHAT IS THE HEART DOING?

Blood always travels around your heart in the same way. It arrives in the top chambers (atria) first, valves open to the bottom chambers (ventricles), and they pump it to the body or lungs. Draw lines to match each illustration with the correct text.

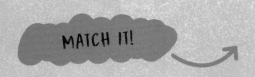

MATCH IT!

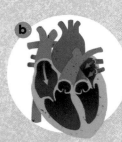

Relax
The heart relaxes, and blood flows in from the body or lungs.

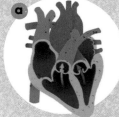

Squeeze
The atrium walls squeeze blood into the chambers below.

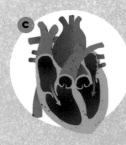

Push
The ventricle walls contract, pumping blood to the body or lungs.

41

IN THE BLOOD

Blood looks red, but actually it is made up of three types of cells—red blood cells, white blood cells, and platelets—all suspended in a yellow liquid called plasma. Blood is vital for many reasons, including transporting oxygen, nutrients, and hormones around the body. It also fights germs and takes away waste.

Red blood cells
These cells carry oxygen around the body.

White blood cells
They help your body defend against disease.

Platelets
These cells help with blood clotting.

Blood breakdown
A child weighing 80 lb (35 kg) has around 5.5 pints (2.5 liters) of blood flowing through their body. Just over half of your blood is plasma, while the rest is made up of blood cells and platelets.

MATCH THE CELLS
The structures of the cells and other materials in your blood are suited to the jobs they do. Can you match each picture to its description?

a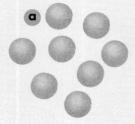

b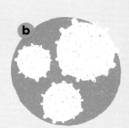

c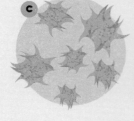

d

MATCH IT!

White blood cells
Irregular in shape, these cells help fight infection and other diseases.

Red blood cells
These are round with a dent in the middle to hold the maximum amount of oxygen.

Plasma
Mostly water, plasma holds cells, proteins, hormones, and other molecules.

Platelets
These small cell fragments clump together to help blood clot.

Blood groups

There are four main blood groups: A, B, AB, and O. If someone needs blood after an accident or surgery, doctors must make sure that the donor blood is a match. If it is not, the white blood cells of the person receiving the blood will think it is a harmful invader and attack it. Here's who can donate blood to each blood group.

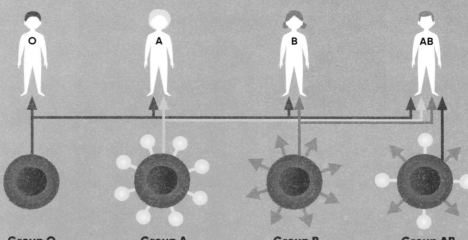

Group O
This donor can give blood to groups O, A, B, and AB.

Group A
This donor can give blood to groups A and AB.

Group B
This donor can give blood to groups B and AB.

Group AB
This donor can only give blood to group AB.

WHO CAN HAVE THE BLOOD?

These bags of donor blood can only be given to people with certain blood groups. Follow the tubes and write who can safely receive the blood from each one.

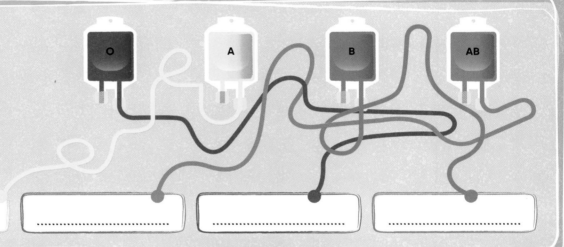

....

COLOR THE LAYERS

Approximately 55 percent of blood is made up of plasma, 44 percent is red blood cells, and 1 percent is white blood cells. Each layer in the test tube represents one of the three parts of blood. Can you color in the correct amount to represent the parts listed in the coloring key below?

Coloring key

〰️ Plasma

〰️ White blood cells

〰️ Red blood cells

COLOR IT!

RED BLOOD CELLS CIRCULATE IN THE BODY FOR ABOUT **4 MONTHS,** WHILE SOME WHITE BLOOD CELLS CAN ONLY SURVIVE FOR **A FEW DAYS.**

THE URINARY SYSTEM

When the body needs to clean your blood, it calls on the urinary system to do the job. Blood is filtered through two bean-shaped organs called the kidneys, which remove excess water, salts, and other things your body doesn't need. These are then sent to your bladder to be passed out of your body as urine (pee).

UNSCRAMBLE THEM

Look at the illustration and labels on the right, showing how the urinary system cleans your blood and gets rid of the waste. Now, unscramble the letters in the circles below to find key parts of the urinary system.

a ....

b ....

c ....

d ....

e ....

FILL IT IN!

YOUR KIDNEYS **FILTER** ALL YOUR BLOOD **40** TIMES EACH **DAY.**

Nephrons
Each kidney has more than 1 million nephrons, microscopic filtering units that clean your blood and balance the body's fluid levels.

Kidneys
Blood flows into the kidneys from the heart, is cleaned, and then is sent back again.

Ureters
These two tubes (one on each side) carry urine from your kidneys to your bladder.

Bladder
This stretchy bag expands to store urine until it is convenient for you to release it.

Urethra
Urine leaves the body via a tube called the urethra (not to be confused with the ureters, above).

44

COLOR THE KIDNEY

Use the key to color the right side of the illustration below to match the left side.

Coloring key

1. Kidney
2. Ureter
3. Bladder
4. Urethra

1

1

1

2

3

COLOR IT!

FILTER THE BLOOD

All day and night, your kidneys are busy filtering blood. Blood from the heart flows into each kidney via a renal artery. Once inside, nephrons remove excess water and waste and make urine. Clean blood flows back to the heart, and urine goes to your bladder. Add numbers to the diagram below to show how the process works.

1 Blood for cleaning
The renal artery carries blood into the kidney.

2 Entering the nephrons
Smaller blood vessels carry blood into the nephrons, located in the outer layer (cortex).

3 Filtration
Waste and water are removed from the blood. Cleaned blood goes back to the heart in veins.

4 Urine collection
The waste is passed to "pyramids" in the inner section, which contain collecting tubes.

5 Renal pelvis
Urine from all the pyramids is fed to this chamber, which leads to the ureter.

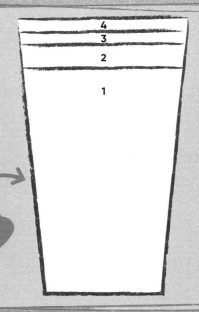

FILL IT IN!

WHAT IS URINE MADE OF?

Most of your urine is water, but it also contains things your body needs to get rid of. Urea (which gives your pee its yellow color) comes from the liver and is a result of the breakdown of proteins and old red blood cells. A high level of salts in your body is harmful, so the kidneys balance this. Color in the measuring glass based on the key below.

4
3
2
1

COLOR ME IN!

Coloring key

1. Water 95%
2. Urea 3%
3. Excess salt 1%
4. Other waste 1%

45

THE DIGESTIVE SYSTEM

The food you eat goes on a pretty long journey through your body. That journey involves chewing, swallowing, digesting, and absorbing before making its final exit. The digestive system is made up of many parts that work together to break down your food, extract the nutrients, and get rid of waste.

FOOD TRAVELS **30 FT** (9 M) ON ITS DIGESTIVE **JOURNEY!**

 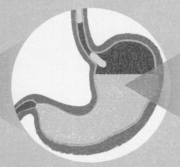  

1 Swallowing
In the mouth, food is chewed up and mixed with saliva, which starts to break it down and helps it slide down the throat into the esophagus.

2 Digesting
In the stomach, food is churned and squeezed by strong muscles in the stomach walls and broken down by enzymes and stomach acid.

3 Absorbing
The broken-down food passes into the small intestine. As it makes its way through, nutrients are absorbed into the blood through the intestinal walls.

4 Leaving
Once the nutrients have been absorbed, the waste passes into the large intestine. Water is extracted, and the waste exits your body.

Villi
Millions of villi line the walls of the small intestine.

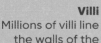

SPOT THE DIFFERENCE
The walls of the small intestine are covered with tiny finger-shaped villi. They absorb nutrients from food, which is then carried to the rest of the body. Spot and circle the three differences between these two pictures of villi.

CIRCLE IT!

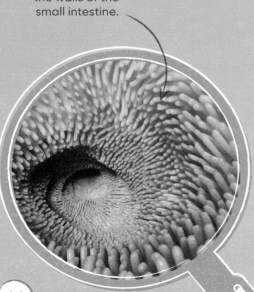

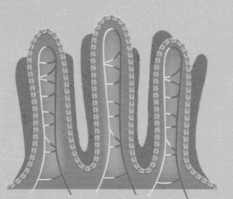

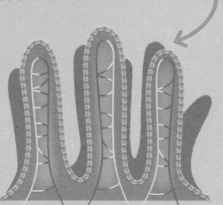

QUIZ YOURSELF!

How much have you learned about the digestive system? Let's find out! Choose the correct answers.

CHECK IT!

a What role do enzymes play in digestion?
- [ ] Cleaning intestines
- [ ] Breaking down food
- [ ] Churning and squeezing food

b Where does food go after leaving the stomach?
- [ ] Small intestine
- [ ] Large intestine
- [ ] Medium intestine

c What does the body absorb from food?
- [ ] Bacteria
- [ ] Waste
- [ ] Nutrients

d How long does it take to digest your food?
- [ ] Less than 20 minutes
- [ ] At least 24 hours
- [ ] 8 hours

DO THE MATH!

It can take between 24 and 72 hours to fully digest food. This person's body takes 24 hours. Color in the diagram to show when an evening meal eaten at 6pm might reach each part of the digestive system. Hint: It spends longest in the large intestine.

Coloring key
- 6–6:30pm
- 6:30–10pm
- 10pm–3am
- 3am–6pm

COLOR IT!

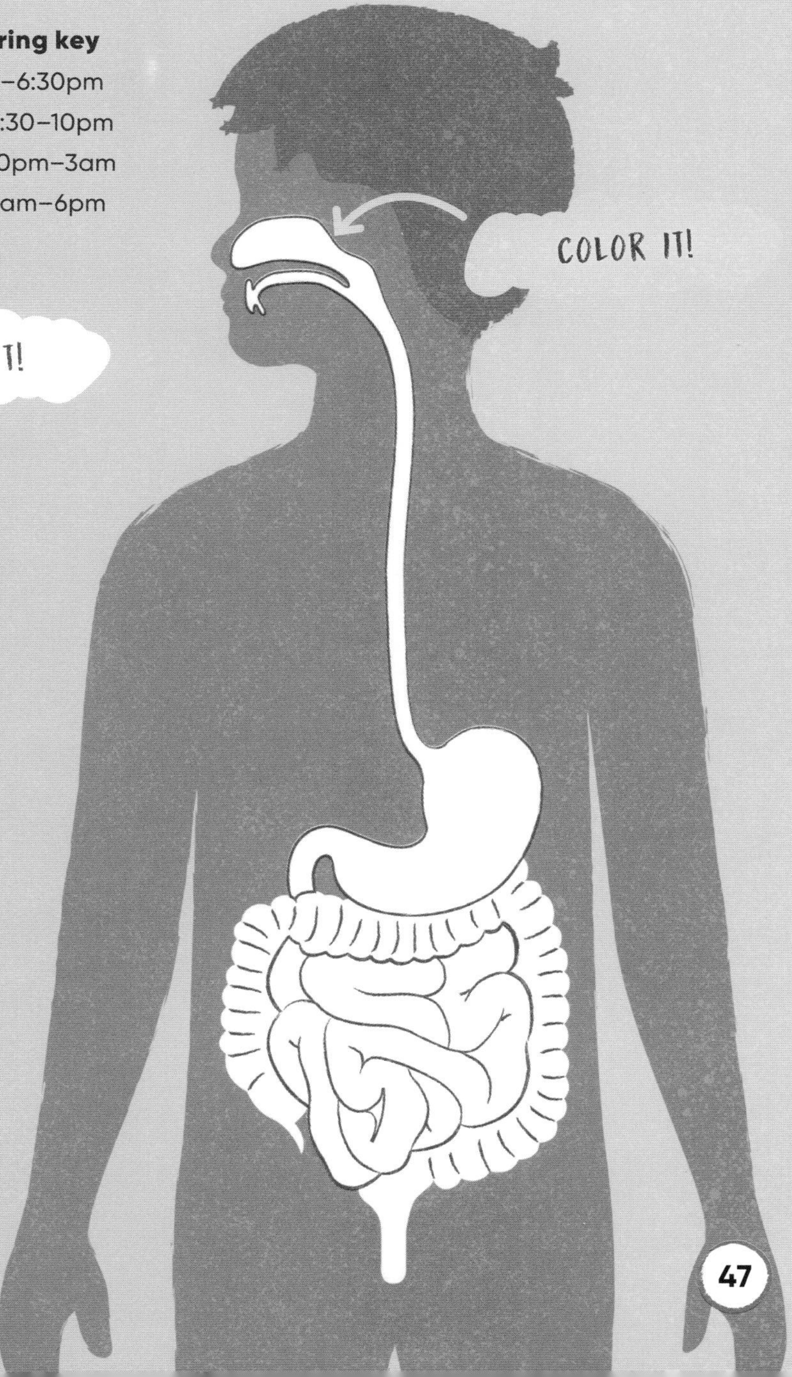

MATCH IT!

WHICH IS WHICH?

Can you match these pictures to the correct moment in our food's journey through the body?

a

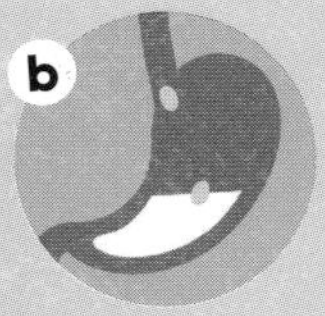

b

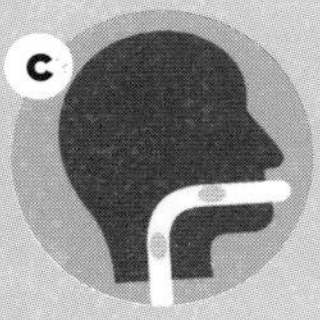

c

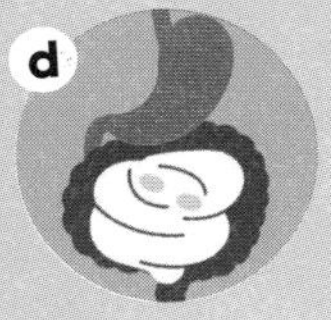

d

Swallowing
The ball (bolus) of chewed food leaves your mouth.

Absorbing
Nutrients from food are absorbed by villi into your blood.

Digesting
The food is broken down by muscles, enzymes, and acid.

Leaving
Any waste that your body doesn't need leaves as poo.

TALES OF YOUR TEETH

Open wide! Your teeth are like a little set of tools inside your mouth. You use them to cut, slice, tear, and chew your food. Without even realizing it, you move food around your mouth so the correct type of teeth can help break it down.

Tooth types

There are four types of teeth: incisors, canines, premolars, and molars. They each have a unique shape that helps them do their specific job. Between them all, there is no food they can't handle!

Incisors
These have sharp edges to cut your food.

Canines
These pointy teeth help tear food.

Premolars
Their two ridges grip food for grinding and help pass it back to the molars.

Molars
These have four ridges for crushing and grinding food.

Enamel
It covers the teeth and protects them from damage.

Dentine
This helps absorb shock while you chew.

Pulp
A soft tissue, this contains nerves and blood vessels.

Gum
This soft tissue covers where teeth lie in the jawbone.

Jawbone
This is a part of the skull.

Nerves and blood vessels
They run between the tooth and the rest of the body.

LABEL THE PARTS

Can you label the different parts of the tooth?

Blood vessels
Pulp
Gum
Dentine
Enamel
Jawbone

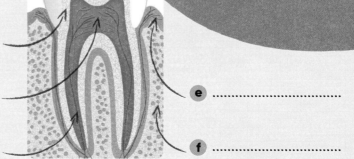

a ....

b ....

c ....

d ....

e ....

f ....

DO THE TEETH-OKU
Can you fill in this puzzle? Each row, column, and box should contain one of each type of tooth.

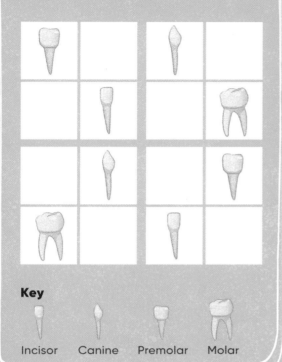

Key

Incisor   Canine   Premolar   Molar

IDENTIFY THE TEETH
Can you match each type of tooth with its description?

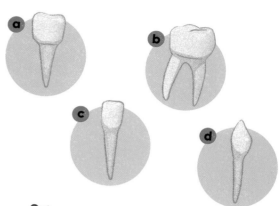

a
b
c
d

Cut
Sharp, straight edges help cut and slice food into smaller pieces.

Tear
Their sharp and pointy shape helps tear tough food apart.

Grip and grind
Flat with two ridges, these teeth grip food as well as grinding it into mush.

Crush and grind
Flat with four small bumps, these back teeth are the largest and strongest.

MATCH IT!

TOOTH ENAMEL IS THE **TOUGHEST** SUBSTANCE IN YOUR BODY, STRONGER THAN **BONES!**

WHICH ARE WHICH?
Using the key below, color the different types of teeth on the permanent set. The picture on the left will help you.

Coloring key
- Molar
- Premolar
- Canine
- Incisor

Baby teeth
Your first set of teeth, known as baby teeth, includes just 20 teeth.

Permanent teeth
Baby teeth start to fall out around age six. By the time you are an adult, you will usually have 32 permanent teeth.

COLOR IT!

GUT REACTIONS

Digestion begins in the mouth, but it really gets going in the stomach—a stretchy bag in the upper-left side of your tummy area. Here, food can stay for up to four hours while special juices break it down into smaller pieces that your body can use.

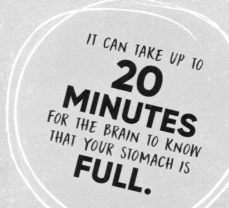

IT CAN TAKE UP TO **20 MINUTES** FOR THE BRAIN TO KNOW THAT YOUR STOMACH IS **FULL.**

Into the stomach

After you swallow, food travels down the esophagus into the stomach. Once inside, the food is churned up by strong muscles and broken down by gastric juices released from cells in the stomach lining.

FROM THE MOUTH

Esophagus
Muscles squeeze to push the food down this tube to your stomach.

Three muscle layers
Strong muscles squeeze in three directions to mash food and push it along.

Stomach lining
This contains special cells that make gastric juices.

Pyloric sphincter
This ring of muscles opens to let the "food soup" into your small intestine.

Chyme
Food mixed with digestive enzymes and acid becomes a soupy mush.

COLOR IT!

FINISH THE ZOOM-IN

Gastric pits in the stomach lining contain different cells. Some make acid to break down food, others make pepsin (an enzyme to digest protein), and some make mucus to protect your stomach lining. Color in the rest of the picture to match.

Food

Pepsin

Gastric pit

Mucus layer

JUICE & SHAKE BAR

Strawberry smoothie
8½ fl oz (250ml)

Orange juice
7⅔ fl oz (225ml)

Can of cola
330ml (11⅕ fl oz)

Banana milk
8⅘ fl oz (260ml)

HOW MANY DRINKS?
An adult stomach can expand from holding less than a cupful of fluid to taking in around 7 pints (4 liters). On the card, color in as many drinks as can fit into a full adult stomach. Don't try to drink all this yourself! Hint: There are 16 fl oz in a pint (1,000 ml in a liter).

COLOR IT!

The pH scale
Stomach acid breaks down food and kills harmful bacteria. We measure the acidity of a substance on the pH scale, which goes from 0 (very acidic) to 14 (very alkaline). Universal indicator strips show pH values as a rainbow of colors. Never drink very acidic or very alkaline substances, as they are toxic.

HOW ACIDIC IS STOMACH ACID?
Solve this math puzzle and find out where stomach acid fits on the pH scale.

The pH of stomach acid is usually between

$$(2.5 + 5) \div 5 \text{ and } (3 \times 7) \div 6$$

.... and ....

WRITE IT!

Battery acid

Lemon

Water

Toothpaste

Bleach

| 0 | 1 | 2 | 3 | 4 | 5 | 6 | 7 | 8 | 9 | 10 | 11 | 12 | 13 | 14 |

ACID **NEUTRAL** **ALKALI**

NUTRITION

Nutrition is the food humans eat to stay alive. To be healthy, our food must contain nutrients —special substances that our bodies need to grow, fight infections, repair damaged cells, get energy, and ensure the organs work properly. No single food contains all the nutrients we need, so it's important to eat a wide variety.

ALL PARTS OF A **PROTEIN-RICH EGG** ARE EDIBLE—EVEN ITS **SHELL!**

Food groups

Nutrients are divided into five main groups: protein, carbohydrates, lipids (fats and oils), vitamins, and minerals. To get the right amount of these nutrients, we need to eat a balanced diet. We also need fiber and water.

Carbohydrates
Found in bread, pasta, potatoes, and grains (rice and cereal), these provide fuel for cells and energy for movement.

Fiber
Fruit and vegetables are high in fiber, which is not digested but helps food move through the gut.

Protein
Beans, eggs, fish, meat, and milk contain protein, which is needed for growth and repair of cells.

Lipids
Fats—from dairy products (butter and cheese) and oils from seeds and fish—store energy.

Vitamins
Small amounts of 13 different vitamins (A, C, D, E, K, and eight B vitamins) help keep us healthy.

Minerals
We need 16 minerals, including calcium and iron, for healthy bones, teeth, blood, and organs.

SORT LIFE'S ESSENTIALS

Match the food groups listed in the box below to the pictures and descriptions of the jobs they do in the body. Write the correct name beside the letters.

> Vitamins   Protein
> Carbohydrates
> Minerals   Lipids   Fiber

WRITE IT!

a ....
We don't digest this food group, but it helps keep the digestive system working properly.

b ....
We need 13 types of this food group for things like good eyesight, healthy skin, and fighting infections.

FILL YOUR PLATE

Different countries recommend different proportions of the food groups. Pick one of the countries and draw a balanced meal on the plate below. Look at the food on the table on the left to help you think of things to draw.

Key

- Dairy
- Protein
- Vegetables
- Fruit
- Carbohydrates
- Sugar
- Lipids

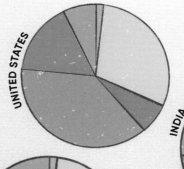
UNITED STATES

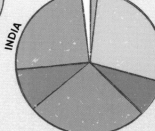
INDIA

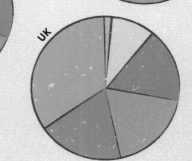
CHINA

UK

DRAW IT!

DECODE THE MESSAGE

Can you read what this back-to-front sentence says? (Hint: use a mirror!) Write the nutritional fact underneath it.

DRINKING ORANGE JUICE WITH YOUR BEANS HELPS YOU ABSORB THEIR IRON.

....
....
....

c ....

Calcium and iron are among these 16 nutrients needed for healthy teeth, bones, blood, and organs.

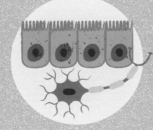

d ....

This food group supplies large amounts of energy that the body can store and keeps the body warm.

e ....

This food group works like quick fuel and is used to provide body cells with energy (respiration).

f ....

This is the building block for all new cells in the body during growth, repair, and maintenance.

24-hour workshop

All your blood passes through the liver, which stores chemicals from food, such as iron, vitamins, and glucose (as glycogen), and removes bad substances.

TO THE HEART

THERE ARE UP TO **1 MILLION** LOBULES (TINY WORKER UNITS) INSIDE YOUR LIVER.

Inferior vena cava
This vein carries clean, low-oxygen blood from the liver to the heart.

Right lobe
The liver has two main sections, and this is the bigger one.

Hepatic portal vein
This carries nutrient-rich, low-oxygen blood from the small intestine to the liver.

Gallbladder
Bile is stored here and released into the small intestine to help digest fat.

Large intestine
This lies in front of the small intestine as it crosses the abdomen.

Left lobe
This is the smaller of the two main sections of the liver.

Stomach
The food you eat is broken down here with stomach acid.

Hepatic artery
This carries oxygen-rich blood from the heart to the liver.

Small intestine
This intestine works with the liver to absorb nutrients into the bloodstream.

THE LIVER

The liver is the largest organ inside your body and an important part of the digestive system. It breaks down and stores nutrients from food and makes a green juice called bile that helps you digest fat. It also cleans your blood by neutralizing poisons and bacteria as well as balancing hormones (chemical messengers).

FINISH THE PICTURE

Look at this body. Which organ is the liver? Color it in. Now, color in the heart, lungs, stomach, and intestines. Look back at pages 36–47 if you are unsure which is which.

Coloring key
- Liver
- Heart
- Lungs
- Stomach
- Intestines

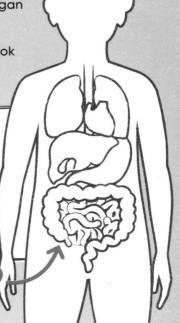

COLOR IT!

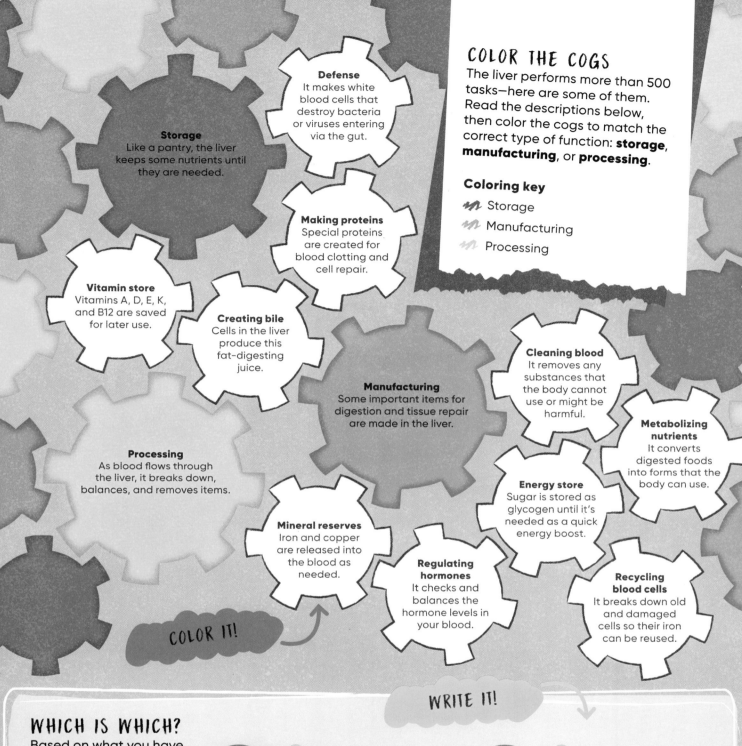

Defense
It makes white blood cells that destroy bacteria or viruses entering via the gut.

Storage
Like a pantry, the liver keeps some nutrients until they are needed.

COLOR THE COGS
The liver performs more than 500 tasks—here are some of them. Read the descriptions below, then color the cogs to match the correct type of function: **storage**, **manufacturing**, or **processing**.

Coloring key
🐟 Storage
🐟 Manufacturing
🐟 Processing

Making proteins
Special proteins are created for blood clotting and cell repair.

Vitamin store
Vitamins A, D, E, K, and B12 are saved for later use.

Creating bile
Cells in the liver produce this fat-digesting juice.

Manufacturing
Some important items for digestion and tissue repair are made in the liver.

Cleaning blood
It removes any substances that the body cannot use or might be harmful.

Metabolizing nutrients
It converts digested foods into forms that the body can use.

Processing
As blood flows through the liver, it breaks down, balances, and removes items.

Energy store
Sugar is stored as glycogen until it's needed as a quick energy boost.

Mineral reserves
Iron and copper are released into the blood as needed.

Regulating hormones
It checks and balances the hormone levels in your blood.

Recycling blood cells
It breaks down old and damaged cells so their iron can be reused.

COLOR IT!

WRITE IT!

WHICH IS WHICH?
Based on what you have learned so far, can you match these descriptions to the correct organs?

Small intestine

Heart   Liver

Gallbladder

a ....
It receives oxygen-rich blood from the heart via the hepatic artery.

b ....
It sends nutrient-rich blood to the liver for processing.

c ....
It releases bile into the small intestine to help break down fat.

d ....
It receives blood that is low in oxygen from the liver after it has been cleaned.

SKIN, HAIR, AND NAILS

Your skin is an organ—your biggest organ, in fact! It's made up of lots of different cells that all have a part to play in protecting your body, regulating your temperature, and providing your sense of touch.

Unique you
How your skin looks and feels depends on many things, including pigmentation, oil, and hair follicles. Whatever your skin type, your skin has exactly the same job to do!

LOOK UNDER YOUR SKIN
The skin has three layers: the epidermis, dermis, and hypodermis. Each layer performs specific functions and contains different cells. Use the key to color this picture and learn more about what happens under your skin!

1 Epidermis
This thin, waterproof, outer layer of skin protects the two layers beneath.

2 Dermis
This thicker layer contains nerve receptor cells, blood vessels, and sweat glands.

3 Sebaceous gland
This makes an oily substance that keeps your hair and skin healthy.

4 Hair
Each hair is made up of the root below the skin and the shaft above.

5 Hair follicles
These are pockets lined with special skin cells that produce hairs.

6 Artery
This vessel carries blood through the skin, supplying it with oxygen.

7 Vein
This vessel carries blood away from the skin, back to the heart.

8 Sweat gland
These small organs produce sweat that cools the skin down.

9 Hypodermis
This bottom layer of fat cells keeps the body warm and cushions it from harm.

COLOR IT!

AN ADULT'S **SKIN** WOULD COVER AN AREA OF **16–21 SQUARE FEET** (1.5–2 SQUARE METERS)!

HOW ABOUT YOU?

Your hair type is determined by the shape of your hair follicles. What type of hair follicles do you have? Draw your own hair on the figure.

Hair follicle shape

DRAW IT!

CURLY

WAVY

STRAIGHT

COILED

LABEL THE NAIL

Both hair and nails are made from a protein called keratin, produced by skin cells. Label this diagram of a nail, using the descriptions to help you.

Nail	Nail bed
Cuticle	Nail root

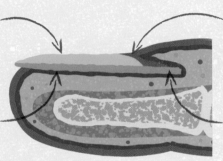

a ....
This hard plate made of keratin protects the tip of your finger.

b ....
This is the skin on which the nail rests. It contains blood vessels and nerves.

c ....
This fold of skin at the base of the nail protects it as it grows

d ....
This hidden part of the nail, under the cuticle, is where growth occurs.

Pigmentation

Skin gets its color from melanin, released by melanocyte cells in the epidermis. The more you have, the darker your skin will be.

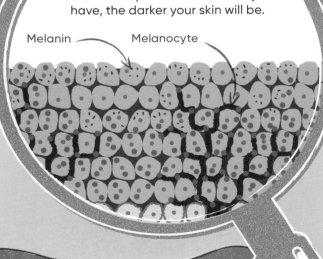

Melanin — Melanocyte

WHICH IS WHICH?

Hairs are made inside follicles. But they don't grow constantly. Each follicle makes hairs and then rests in between. Match the stages to the words below.

MATCH IT!

 **a**

 **b**

 **c**

Resting stage
The follicle gets narrower. The hair stops growing, pulls away from the root, and falls out.

New growth
The cycle begins. As we age, fewer follicles reactivate to grow new hairs, so our hair appears thinner.

Active follicle
New cells are made inside the hair root. As these die, the hair is pushed up to form a long shaft.

THE MALE REPRODUCTIVE SYSTEM

The main function of the male reproductive system is to make sperm, which, when joined with a female egg, can make a baby. At puberty, changes occur in the body that prepare a boy to become a father. Sex hormones are released that begin the manufacture of sperm inside the testes and cause the penis and all the accompanying organs to develop.

IT TAKES ABOUT **2.5 MONTHS** FOR EACH SPERM TO BECOME **FULLY MATURE.**

SPERM

With its streamlined shape, each sperm is designed to swim toward a female egg.

Head
This contains genetic code from the male.

Know your male parts
The visible parts of the reproductive system are the penis and scrotum, but there are vital bits hidden inside too. These organs, glands, and tubes make, store, and transport sperm to the penis.

Seminal vesicle
These make seminal fluids that protect and nourish sperm.

BLADDER

Tail
Once the sperm has entered the egg, the tail drops off.

Sperm duct
This tube links the epididymis to the urethra.

Prostate
This makes seminal fluids, and helps eject semen and sperm from the urethra.

Urethra
Semen and sperm travel down this tube inside the penis.

Penis
It is used for reproduction and peeing, but never at the same time.

Epididymis
Each of these coiled tubes stores sperm while they mature.

Scrotum
This stretchy, pouchlike structure is where the testes hang.

Testis
Each one of these organs can produce millions of sperm.

Foreskin
Boys are born with this flap of skin over the tip of the penis.

A sperm's journey

The testes are making sperm all the time. The sperm leave the testes as small, round cells and move into the epididymis to mature into their characteristic "tadpole" shape. They then travel to the penis in semen, a nutrient-rich fluid.

LABEL IT!

Using the word pool below, write the correct label above each description on the diagram.

Sperm duct

Urethra

Seminal vesicle

Penis

Epididymis

.... **a**

Semen is produced here. It contains nutrients for the sperm.

.... **b**

The sperm travel along this tube (duct), past the bladder, to the urethra.

.... **c**

This organ allows the sperm to enter the female body during sexual intercourse.

.... **d**

Semen and millions of sperm travel down this tube and leave the body.

.... **e**

This is where the sperm develop into fully formed reproductive cells.

SPOT THE CHANGES

The testes are not just a part of the male reproductive system—they are part of the endocrine system too. At puberty, the testes start producing a male hormone called testosterone, which causes major changes in a boy's body. Draw a line from each description to the correct picture.

MATCH IT!

Voice
The voice deepens, which is sometimes called "breaking."

Facial and body hair
Hair starts to grow on the body, particularly around the genitals and on the face.

Growth and strength
The bones grow and thicken, and the muscles increase in size.

THE FEMALE REPRODUCTIVE SYSTEM

During puberty, the female body changes to prepare for reproduction (having a baby). Eggs start maturing inside the ovaries, and a monthly cycle begins in the uterus (womb), which creates the conditions for a baby to grow. This only happens if a female egg joins with a male sperm. If it doesn't, a period takes place.

THE OVARIES ALREADY CONTAIN 1–2 MILLION EGGS AT BIRTH.

EGG
Also called an ovum, this cell contains the mother's genetic information.

On the inside (front view)

Most of the female reproductive organs are inside the body. Each month, an egg is released from one of the two ovaries and travels to the uterus. If fertilized by a sperm, it can develop into a baby.

Fallopian tube
A tube joins each ovary to the uterus. Sperm meet the egg here.

Uterus (womb)
This small, muscular organ is where a baby grows during pregnancy.

Cervix
This opening to the uterus allows sperm in and the baby out.

Ovary
These two organs store eggs, taking turns to release a mature one every month.

Vagina
This muscular tube leads from the cervix to outside the body.

On the outside (lying down)

The external parts of the female reproductive system are called the vulva. The vulva protects the vagina from infection and stimulates the body for sexual intercourse.

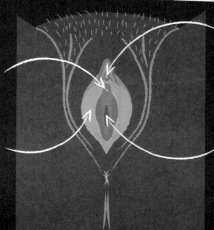

Urethra
Pee leaves the body from here. It plays no role in reproduction.

Labia
These flaps of skin, or lips, protect the vagina and urethra.

Clitoris
If the clitoris is stimulated by touch, the vagina becomes ready for intercourse.

Vaginal opening
The male penis enters here, and the baby is born from here.

An egg's journey

A female baby is born with all her eggs. After puberty, an egg matures each month and is released from one of the ovaries. It then travels down the fallopian tube to the uterus and is either fertilized by a sperm and becomes a baby or is shed during a period.

LABEL IT!

Using the word pool below, write the correct label above each description on the diagram (right).

> Ovary   Uterus
>
> Fallopian tube
>
> Egg

WRITE IT!

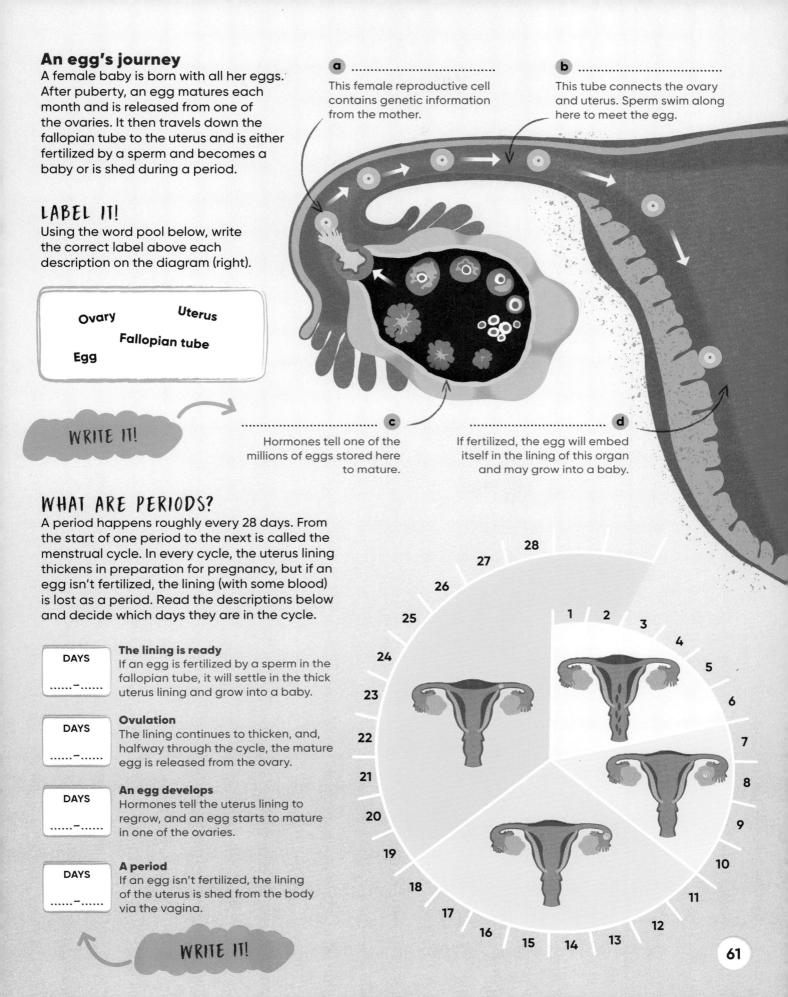

a ....
This female reproductive cell contains genetic information from the mother.

b ....
This tube connects the ovary and uterus. Sperm swim along here to meet the egg.

c ....
Hormones tell one of the millions of eggs stored here to mature.

d ....
If fertilized, the egg will embed itself in the lining of this organ and may grow into a baby.

WHAT ARE PERIODS?

A period happens roughly every 28 days. From the start of one period to the next is called the menstrual cycle. In every cycle, the uterus lining thickens in preparation for pregnancy, but if an egg isn't fertilized, the lining (with some blood) is lost as a period. Read the descriptions below and decide which days they are in the cycle.

DAYS ...... - ......
The lining is ready
If an egg is fertilized by a sperm in the fallopian tube, it will settle in the thick uterus lining and grow into a baby.

DAYS ...... - ......
Ovulation
The lining continues to thicken, and, halfway through the cycle, the mature egg is released from the ovary.

DAYS ...... - ......
An egg develops
Hormones tell the uterus lining to regrow, and an egg starts to mature in one of the ovaries.

DAYS ...... - ......
A period
If an egg isn't fertilized, the lining of the uterus is shed from the body via the vagina.

WRITE IT!

Fertilization

A male makes millions of sperm, but only one joins with the female egg. Both the sperm and egg are specially designed to ensure this happens. The reproductive cells (gametes) contain genetic code from the parents, which combines to create a totally unique baby.

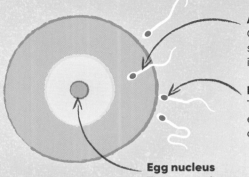

A sperm enters
Chemicals on the sperm head help it enter the egg.

No more sperm can enter
The outer layer of the egg hardens to block other sperm.

Egg nucleus
The sperm fuses with the nucleus of the egg. Together, they become a cluster of cells that develops into a baby.

Twins

Two babies sometimes develop inside the mother's uterus—these are known as twins. This can happen in two different ways and results in either identical or non-identical (fraternal) twins.

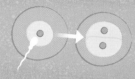

Identical twins
An egg divides in half immediately after fertilization to create two babies with identical genes.

Non-identical twins
Two eggs are fertilized by two sperm. They are no more alike than other brothers and sisters.

WHICH SPERM?

Lots of sperm cells swim toward the egg cell, but only one can get through. Unravel the sperm tangle to find out which of these sperm cells will reach the egg cell and fertilize it.

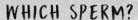
FIND IT!

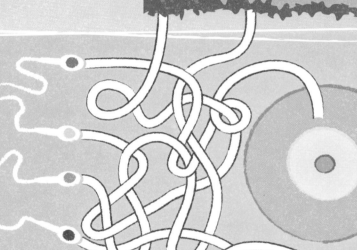

PREGNANCY

After the fertilization of a female egg by a male sperm, a human baby takes about nine months to develop. From a single cell that divides and replicates, the fetus (made up of trillions of cells) is nourished and protected in the mother's uterus until it is ready to be born. This time inside the mother is known as pregnancy, which is divided into three stages, or trimesters.

1 First trimester
In this first stage, the fetus grows rapidly. By week 12, it is about the size of a lemon and is recognizably human. All the internal organs are formed as well as tiny fingers and toes.

AT 12 WEEKS

Breasts

Humans are mammals, which means they give birth to live young (unlike birds, which lay eggs) and can feed their babies with mother's milk. During pregnancy, the breasts change in readiness for feeding the baby. Inside each breast, about 15 to 20 sections (lobes) make milk, which travels down ducts to the nipple.

COLOR IT!

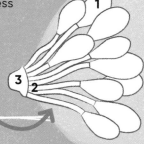

COLOR BY NUMBER
Look at the information on the left and then color in the different parts of the breast, using the coloring key below.

Coloring key
1 Lobes
2 Milk ducts
3 Nipple

Uterus
This amazing expanding organ has muscular walls, which push the baby out during birth.

Amniotic fluid
The liquid inside the sac keeps the fetus warm and cushions it from knocks. It also allows the fetus to stretch its muscles.

Fetus
The fetus drinks amniotic fluid, and its kidneys make pee. It won't breathe air until it is born.

Amniotic sac

Placenta
Attached to the wall of the uterus, this organ transfers nutrients and oxygen from the mother to the baby. It also takes waste away.

Umbilical cord
This coiled tube connects the baby to the placenta.

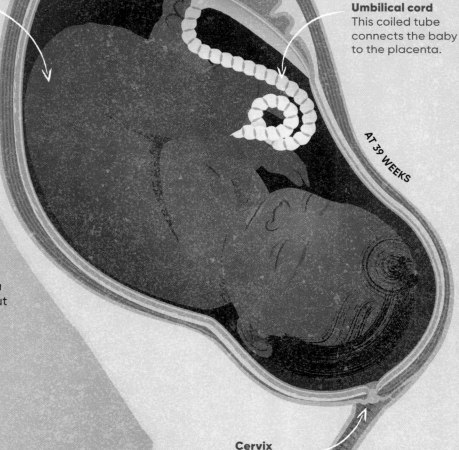

AT 39 WEEKS

3 Third trimester
The final stage of pregnancy is all about the fetus fattening up before birth. The lungs also need to fully mature. By 39 weeks, the fetus has usually turned around, ready to be born head first.

2 Second trimester
In this stage, the organs mature. By week 26, the fetus is about the size of a honeydew melon. Its lungs move in and out in preparation for breathing, its eyes can open, and it may even suck its thumb.

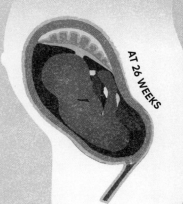

AT 26 WEEKS

Cervix

Birth canal

63

INSTRUCTIONS FOR LIFE

Deoxyribonucleic acid (DNA for short) is what makes you you. It is a chemical stored in each of your cells, and it contains the instructions for your body. These instructions are like a code—a really long code. Everyone's code is different because we are made up of DNA from both of our biological parents.

HUMANS SHARE **60% OF DNA** WITH FRUIT FLIES.

1 Body
Everything about your body—from skin color to earlobe shape to toe length—is determined by your DNA.

2 Cell
In your cells, the nucleus stores your complete DNA within 46 chromosomes, which are grouped into 23 pairs.

3 Chromosome
Chromosomes are tight coils of DNA. Chromosomes contain the DNA instructions for all the parts of your body.

4 DNA
This is a chemical strand made up of molecules known as bases. These bases form the code in your genes.

COLOR THE PAIRS
Chromosomes almost always come in pairs, with the same type of genes on each one. Color in the blank chromosome to look like its matching pair.

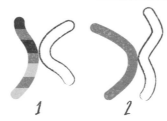

1 *2* *3* *4* *5* *6*

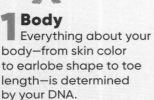

7 *8* *9* *10* *11* *12* *13* *14* *15* *16*

17 *18* *19* *20* *21* *22* *23*

X and Y chromosomes
This pair decides your sex. Males usually have XY and females XX chromosomes.

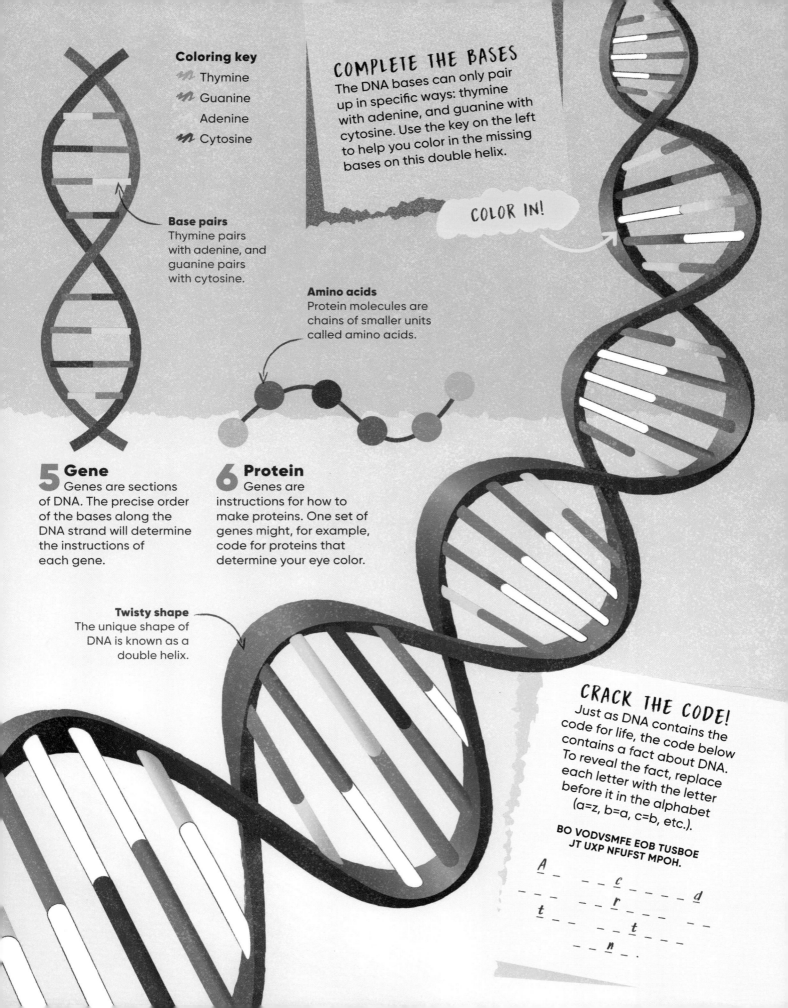

Coloring key
- Thymine
- Guanine
- Adenine
- Cytosine

Base pairs
Thymine pairs with adenine, and guanine pairs with cytosine.

COMPLETE THE BASES
The DNA bases can only pair up in specific ways: thymine with adenine, and guanine with cytosine. Use the key on the left to help you color in the missing bases on this double helix.

COLOR IN!

Amino acids
Protein molecules are chains of smaller units called amino acids.

5 Gene
Genes are sections of DNA. The precise order of the bases along the DNA strand will determine the instructions of each gene.

6 Protein
Genes are instructions for how to make proteins. One set of genes might, for example, code for proteins that determine your eye color.

Twisty shape
The unique shape of DNA is known as a double helix.

CRACK THE CODE!
Just as DNA contains the code for life, the code below contains a fact about DNA. To reveal the fact, replace each letter with the letter before it in the alphabet (a=z, b=a, c=b, etc.).

**BO VODVSMFE EOB TUSBOE
JT UXP NFUFST MPOH.**

A _ _ _ _ _ _ c _ _ _ _ _ d
_ _ _ _ _ r _ _ _ _ _ _
t _ _ _ _ _ _ t _
_ _ _ n _

Stages of life

Humans go through several distinct life stages, from birth to old age. Everyone grows and develops at their own pace, but there are average ages for each stage.

The head is proportionately larger, and arms and legs shorter. Babies don't have the strength to stand up but soon learn to roll or crawl.

The arms and legs grow, so that the head no longer looks large, although the brain is developing rapidly.

Bodily growth slows slightly, but the brain is still developing rapidly as children learn new skills.

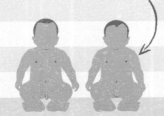

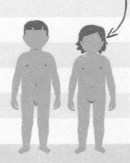

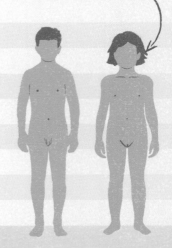

1 Baby (0–1 year)
In the first year, babies are totally dependent on their parents. They communicate by crying when hungry or if their diapers need changing.

2 Toddler (1–3 years)
During this stage, toddlers learn to walk, if unsteadily at first. They also begin to talk—by the age of three, most can say more than 1,000 words.

3 Child (3–10 years)
Play is important for children at this stage, to master such skills as running, jumping, and socializing. Children also learn to read and write.

WHICH STAGE IS WHICH?

Read the descriptions below and decide which life stage from the diagram above they match. Write the numbers in the white circles.

First steps
.... By the end of this stage, you can stand, walk, and speak more than 1,000 words.

School time
.... Your brain is developing fast, you start school, and you learn to make new friends.

All grown up
.... Your body reaches its maximum height. You may want to have children of your own.

Rolling along
.... You need looking after but soon learn to move around by rolling and crawling.

Slowing down
.... Your body works more slowly. Your skin becomes wrinkled, and your hair goes gray.

All change
.... These are the years in which puberty takes place and you become a teenager.

FIND IT!

GROWING UP

From the moment that a sperm and egg cell join, the human body begins to grow. Growth continues after birth until you become an adult, and our brains are continually developing. Over the course of your lifetime, your body undergoes many changes.

AN ADULT BODY MAKES **3.8 MILLION NEW CELLS** EVERY SECOND!

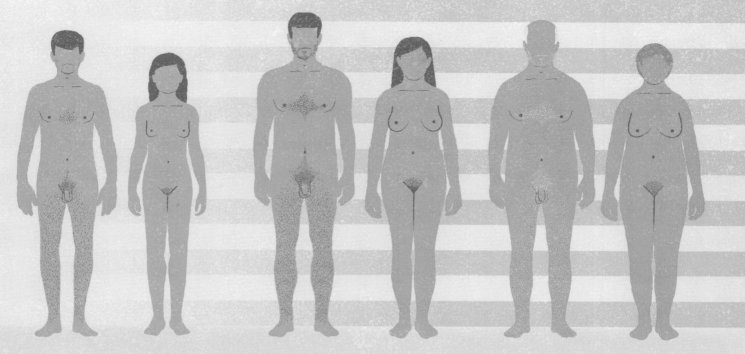

4 **Adolescent (11–18 years)**
Hormones cause puberty to take place. The body changes shape, the reproductive system develops, and hair grows in new places.

5 **Adult (18+ years)**
The body reaches its full height and stops growing, but maintenance continues by replacing old cells and repairing damaged tissues.

6 **Elderly adult (about 60+ years)**
As the body ages, it takes longer to repair and replace its cells. The spine shortens, wrinkles appear, and the hair goes gray or white.

DRAW IT!

DRAW YOURSELF
Draw yourself as you looked as a baby in the first frame, then as you are today. Now, imagine how you might look at ages 40 and 80 and draw these future selves in the other two frames.

As a baby

Now

UNSCRAMBLE THE LIFE STAGE
Cross out the letters that spell "hormone" below. Then, unscramble the remaining letters to spell the teenage event that causes the reproductive system to mature.

O R B O R U H
T E Y M P N E

_ _ _ _ _ _ _

At 40 years old

At 80 years old

WRITE IT!

THE ENDOCRINE SYSTEM

Endocrine glands are all over your body, and their job is to produce chemical messengers known as hormones. Unlike messages sent by the nervous system, which travel very fast, hormones travel more slowly, in the bloodstream, and act over a longer time and wider area.

Hormones zone

Each endocrine gland releases one or more hormones. They travel all over the body but only affect their target tissues or organ. Everyone has the same glands, except males have testes and females have ovaries. The main glands are shown here.

Hypothalamus
This part of the brain controls the whole endocrine system.

Pituitary gland
This "master" gland makes hormones that control other glands.

Thyroid
Thyroxine from here controls conversion of food into energy (your metabolic rate).

Adrenal glands
Adrenaline from these two glands prepares the body for action.

Pancreas
Insulin and glucagon from here regulate blood sugar levels.

Ovary
These two glands make the female sex hormones: estrogen and progesterone.

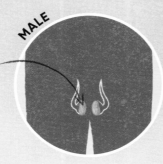

MALE

Testis
These two glands make testosterone, the male sexual hormone.

FEMALE

WHICH IS WHICH?

Join the dots to reveal four endocrine glands, then match the gland to the hormone that it produces below. The picture and labels above will help you.

DRAW IT!

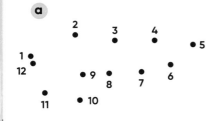

a

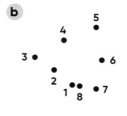

b

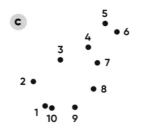

c

d

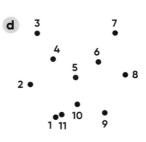

Estrogen   *Thyroxine*   *Insulin*   *Adrenaline*

MATCH IT!

HOW DO WE KNOW WHEN TO SLEEP?

Melatonin and serotonin are our sleep and awake hormones. **Melatonin** is triggered by darkness, and **serotonin** by natural light. Another hormone, **cortisol**, boosts our daytime energy and alertness. Label each picture with the name of the correct hormone.

WRITE IT!

AT DUSK

This hormone starts to make you feel relaxed and sleepy.

....

AT DAWN

This hormone begins to wake up the brain and body.

....

MID-MORNING

This hormone makes your mind and body feel really alert.

....

FIND THE WORDS

Known as the flight-or-fight hormone, adrenaline is released by your adrenal glands when you feel scared or excited. Your heart beats faster, sending more oxygen to your brain and muscles. See if you can find all the endocrine glands hiding in the skate park below.

Pituitary gland   Ovary   Pancreas
Hypothalamus
Thyroid   Testis   Adrenal glands

DECODE IT!

The pituitary gland produces a hormone that stimulates human growth and cell repair. Replace each letter below with the one before it in the alphabet to find what the hormone is called.

T P N B U P U S P Q J O

....

FIND IT!

```
                                              L
                                        H     A
                                        Y     R
                                        F  P  W
                                        A  R  O  B
                                        B  W  S  T  J
                                        J  G  T  O  H  N
                              O  U  I  U  H  P  A  T
W D U B                       T P O V D  H  E  Y  J  L  Y
O V A R Y K M I
F G L V B K D E H F Q U F U R F E A U P A N C R E A S
I U C R A D R E N A L G L A N D S K H J S G P O M M J
O N S A V M K O P G H K J J P S I T S E T X M I X U I
P I T U I T A R Y G L A N D Y G Z L W M J V F D W S Q
```

SLEEP

Your body works hard every single second of the day, so it's no wonder it needs a break. Sleep is how your body pauses and recharges so it can continue helping you do everything you want to!

Sleep cycle

Our bodies rest while we sleep, but our brains never stop working! Our sleep comes in cycles of lighter and deeper sleep, and the brain's level of activity changes at each stage.

| 8PM | 9PM | 10PM | 11PM | 12AM | 1AM | 2AM | 3AM | 4AM | 5AM | 6AM | 7AM |

AWAKE

LIGHT During light sleep, your brain activity and heart rate begin to slow down.

DEEP During deep sleep, brain activity picks up again, with both fast and slow brain waves.

REM Rapid eye movement (REM) sleep is when we dream. Our eyes move under our eyelids, and brain activity is high.

WHICH IS WHICH?

What you do affects the type of brain waves you produce. Can you match the brain wave traces to the activities that might be causing them?

MATCH IT!

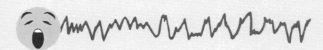

Alpha waves
You are awake but relaxed.

Beta waves
You are awake and alert.

Theta waves
You feel drowsy.

Delta waves
You are in deep or REM sleep.

Benefits of sleep

When we feel tired, we go to sleep. But sleep is so much more than a way for us to feel awake and refreshed. Sleep is a vital function of the human body—we cannot survive without sleep.

Growth
While we sleep, the body uses energy to repair bones and muscles and to make us grow.

Memory
While we sleep, our brain processes the day, storing useful memories and erasing useless ones.

Mood and energy
Getting enough sleep reduces stress, gives you energy, and improves your mood.

Healing
By sleeping, we allow our bodies to use extra energy to heal any parts that are broken or hurt.

HOW MUCH SLEEP DO YOU NEED?

As we grow up, the amount of sleep we need changes. Read the clues below each person to decide how many hours of sleep they need.

1 week old
A 1-week-old baby needs double the amount of sleep a 15-year-old needs.

5 years old
A 5-year-old child needs double its age in hours of sleep.

15 years old
A 15-year-old teenager needs two hours less sleep than a 5-year-old.

50 years old
A 50-year-old adult needs one hour of sleep less than a 15-year-old.

WRITE IT!

a ....   b ....   c ....   d ....

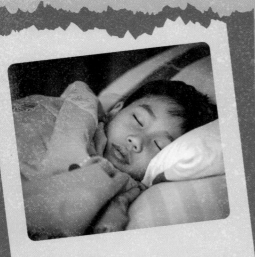

DRAW YOUR LAST DREAM

Some people keep a journal of their dreams, while others forget their dreams as soon as they wake up! Draw the last dream you can remember here.

DRAW IT!

Dreams

Experts still cannot fully explain why we dream. All we know is that dreams are often strange and illogical, but they can include elements from our everyday life. They can sometimes leave us feeling strong emotions.

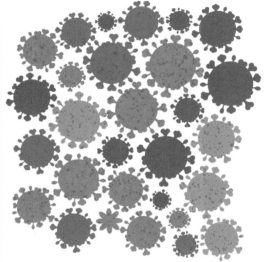

Outer envelope
This layer protects the virus.

Protein shell
This surrounds the genetic material inside the virus.

Genetic material
DNA or RNA are the core part of any virus.

Going viral

A virus is a microbe—a tiny life-form, much smaller than most bacteria. The virus finds a host cell and takes it over by injecting the cell with its genetic code. It then makes the cell produce multiple copies of the virus.

VIRUS INVASION

A virus is tiny but very good at spreading disease throughout your body. It invades your body and uses your own cells to create millions of copies of itself. The copies move on to infect more cells in your body and continue multiplying.

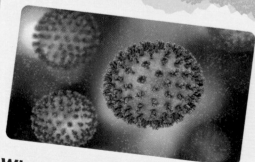

What is a virus?
A virus is a parasite, which means it needs other living cells—called host cells—to copy itself. The cells in our bodies are the hosts.

WHICH IS WHICH?

Viruses come in many different shapes—some of them are incredibly complex! Can you match these viruses to the correct descriptions?

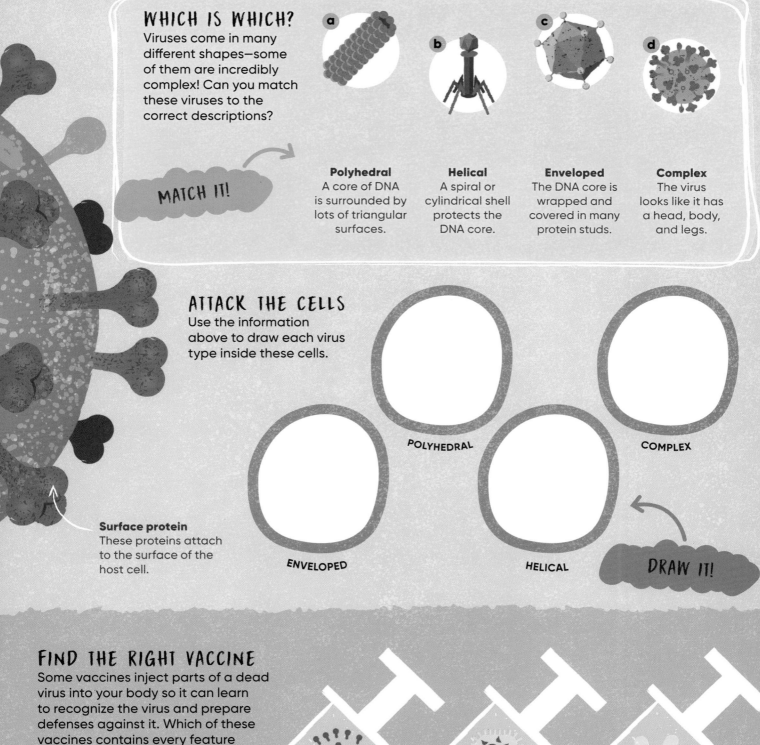

a

b

c

d

MATCH IT!

Polyhedral
A core of DNA is surrounded by lots of triangular surfaces.

Helical
A spiral or cylindrical shell protects the DNA core.

Enveloped
The DNA core is wrapped and covered in many protein studs.

Complex
The virus looks like it has a head, body, and legs.

ATTACK THE CELLS

Use the information above to draw each virus type inside these cells.

POLYHEDRAL

COMPLEX

Surface protein
These proteins attach to the surface of the host cell.

ENVELOPED

HELICAL

DRAW IT!

FIND THE RIGHT VACCINE

Some vaccines inject parts of a dead virus into your body so it can learn to recognize the virus and prepare defenses against it. Which of these vaccines contains every feature of the red virus below?

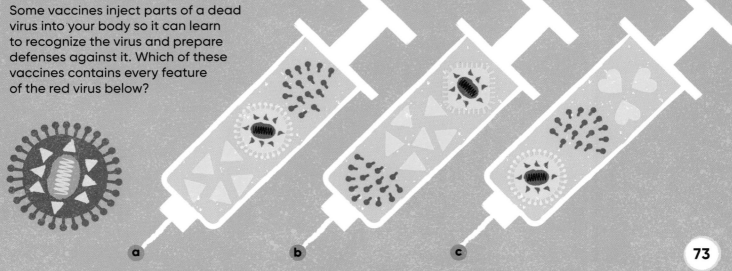

a

b

c

BACTERIA

Bacteria are single-celled organisms, the most basic living things on Earth. Invisible to the naked eye, they exist both in and on the body. Most bacteria are harmless, but there are a few that can make us unwell with things like ear infections and upset stomachs.

Friend and foe

Although some bacteria are harmful, many are helpful to us. For example, bacteria in the gut help us digest our food. Bacteria vary in their shape and size, but they share common features.

Cell membrane
This layer controls which substances can pass in and out of the cell.

Cell wall
This thick outer layer protects the bacteria and gives it shape.

Flagellum
Some bacteria have a long, spinning tail to help them swim.

Plasmids
These small, round pieces of DNA can be passed between bacteria cells.

Cytoplasm
This thick gel inside the cell is where chemical changes occur.

Pili
Some bacteria have little hairs, which they use to attach to surfaces or to each other.

DNA molecule
This long, tangled string has information that tells the cell what to do.

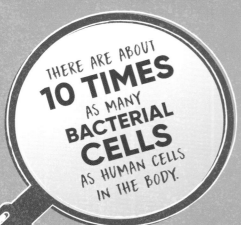

THERE ARE ABOUT **10 TIMES** AS MANY **BACTERIAL CELLS** AS HUMAN CELLS IN THE BODY.

MATCH IT!

WHICH IS WHICH?

Bacteria come in many forms because they thrive in different conditions, often very extreme ones. Draw a line to match the bacterium to its description below.

a b c d e

Spirillum
This water-loving bacterium has a long, thick corkscrew shape.

Vibrio
This saltwater bacterium is recognizable by its curved shape and long tail.

Coccus
Spherical in shape, this bacterium can infect untreated wounds.

Spirochaeta
This thin, spiral-shaped bacterium usually thrives without oxygen.

Bacillus
This cylindrical, rod-shaped bacterium is typically found in soil and water.

COMPLETE IT!

Let's see what you have learned so far! Color in all the parts of this bacterium, using the coloring key on the right.

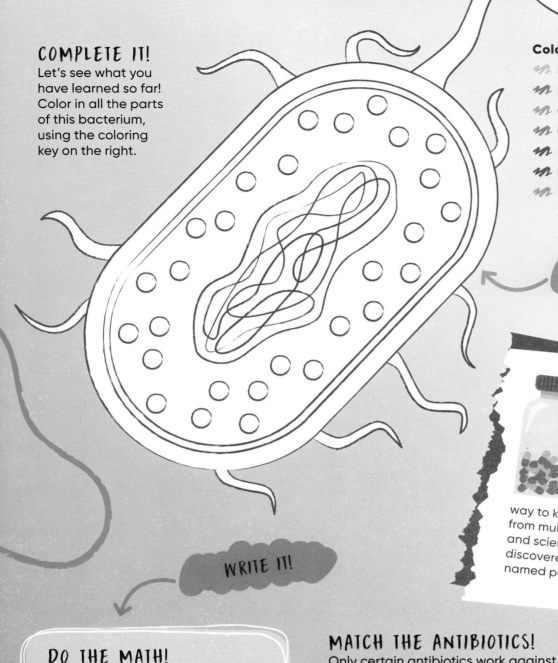

Coloring key

- Plasmids
- DNA molecule
- Cytoplasm
- Cell membrane
- Pili
- Cell wall
- Flagellum

COLOR IT!

Medical miracle

Antibiotics are medicines that help the body fight bacterial infections. Each antibiotic works in a different way to kill bacteria or keep them from multiplying. Scottish doctor and scientist Alexander Fleming discovered the first one, which he named penicillin.

WRITE IT!

DO THE MATH!

Subtract one number from the other below to find out the year in which Alexander Fleming discovered penicillin.

2765 – 837 =

MATCH THE ANTIBIOTICS!

Only certain antibiotics work against certain bacteria, a bit like a key fitting into a lock. Pick the antibiotic that fits each bacterium below and draw a line between the two.

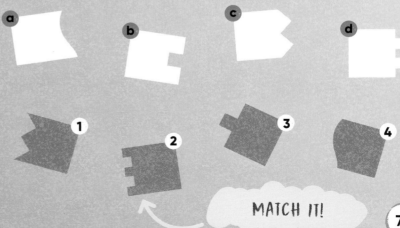

a   b   c   d

1   2   3   4

MATCH IT!

THE IMMUNE SYSTEM

Your immune system protects your body from infection and disease. Whenever something new enters the body, your immune system works hard to identify whether it is harmful. If it is, your clever antibodies and white blood cells will get to work!

IDENTICAL TWINS RARELY END UP WITH EXACTLY THE SAME **IMMUNITY** BECAUSE OUR IMMUNITY IS SHAPED BY WHAT EACH PERSON IS EXPOSED TO.

 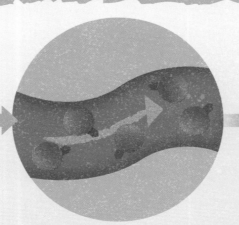 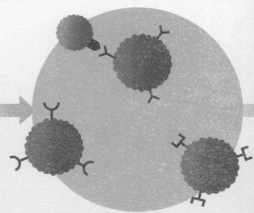

1 Attack
A germ—a virus or a harmful bacterium—invades the body and multiplies. Infection begins to spread.

2 Transport
The germ is carried through the body to a lymph node—a vital part of the immune system.

3 Identify
Antibody cells within the lymph node detect the germ and identify which antibody shape it matches.

SOLVE THE RIDDLE
Many antibodies are shaped like a certain letter of the alphabet. Can you figure out which letter of the alphabet this riddle refers to?

· This letter appears in every day of the week.

It's neither the first nor the last letter of the alphabet.

It does not appear in the word ANTIBODIES.

WRITE IT!

I look like the letter ....

NAME THAT CELL

White blood cells are the body's defense against germs. Cross out the letters of the word IMMUNITY to find a type of white blood cell. Write the answer below.

I P U H A M G
O C M N Y I Y
T T E

FILL IT IN!

_ _ _ _ _ _ _ _ _ _

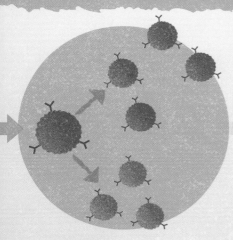

4 Multiply
The matching antibody cell creates many clones (copies) of itself as well as memory cells for the future.

5 Search
The clones release lots of matching antibodies into the bloodstream to fight off the infection.

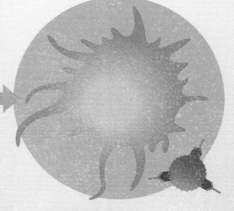

6 Destroy
The antibodies signal white blood cells called phagocytes to come and destroy the germ.

TRACK A GERM'S JOURNEY

Using what you've just learned, can you number these steps to show the journey of a germ?

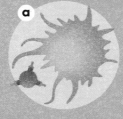

a

Phagocyte
The phagocyte destroys the germ by absorbing it and breaking it down.

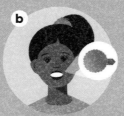

b

Germ
A germ enters the body through a cut or through the eyes, nose, or mouth.

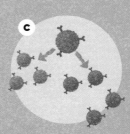

c

Clones
The antibody cell creates clones of itself.

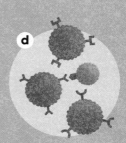

d

Antibody
Antibody cells see which antibody shape matches the germ.

ORGANIZE IT!

 ....

HEALING

Your body has remarkable ways of repairing itself. This goes on daily as part of general maintenance, but also if you cut yourself or break a bone. When this happens, several types of specialized cells spring into action to mend the wound or repair the fracture and keep out harmful germs.

FIND IT!

FIND THE HEALING WORDS
Can you find the words from the word pool below in this letter grid?

J	P	L						N	A	B		
U	P	C	O	S			O	E	M	C	V	
G	I	L	F	E	G		U	N	P	J	I	Z
O	O	S	M	A	M	C	O	L	L	O		
T	A	E	R	E	S	C	A	B				
T	T	S	P	I	K	Y	T					
X	H	K	H	O	N	E						
T	Q	C	Z	A	I	R	L	N				
I	G	F	I	B	R	I	N	E	C	U		
M	N	T	J	L	M		N	I	T	S	O	Z
K	X	S	A				R	A	L	R		
B	O						L	S				

Fibrin   **Mesh**   **Spiky**
Clot   **Platelet**   **Scab**

How a cut heals
The first reaction to a cut is for it to bleed. This can be worrying, but bleeding washes dirt away. Different cells in the blood then begin to heal the cut.

Fibrin strands
The strands stick together to form a net or mesh.

Platelets
These tiny cell fragments live for 5–10 days and can change their shape from round to spiky.

White blood cells
These surround and destroy any germs that may have entered the wound.

Red blood cells
Clotted cells seal the wound, which protects it from further infection.

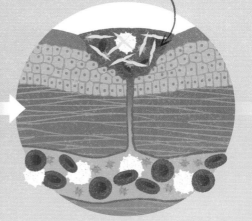

1 Wounded skin
Blood rushes to the site of the injury. It contains three different types of cell needed for healing: red blood cells, white blood cells, and platelets.

2 Emergency!
The platelets suddenly become spiky and release protein strands called fibrin. They also release chemicals that bind the fibrin strands together.

3 Clotting
The red blood cells get caught up in the mesh of fibrin, creating a clot that stops the bleeding. Blood can turn from liquid to solid in just a few minutes.

FILL IT IN

Our bones are strong, but if we hit them hard enough, they can break (fracture). Broken bones are repaired in a different way from skin cuts. Use the word pool on the right to label the healing stages.

a ....
The bone breaks and blood rushes to the break to form a clot. The area may look swollen or bruised.

b ....
About a week after the break, a soft healing tissue called a callus starts to replace the blood clot.

c ....
The callus hardens, and, after 3–4 weeks, new bone cells start to grow at the edges of the two pieces of broken bone.

d ....
New bone cells have totally replaced the callus, and the broken bone is healed—usually within 2–3 months.

Building new skin
The skin heals layer by layer, from the bottom of the cut to the top.

Scab
The scab falls off once the wound has been completely filled with new cells.

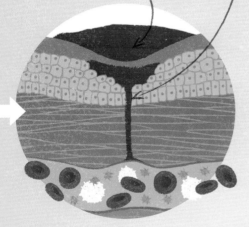

4 Healing skin
The top layer of clotted blood dries to form a crust, or scab, to protect the wound. The skin is healed after about 7–10 days, depending on how deep the cut is.

HEAL THE CUT!

First, draw a net made from fibrin threads. Add three white blood cells, then fill in the rest of the net with platelets and red blood cells. Finally, draw a scab over the top.

Object key
- Red blood cell
- White blood cell
- Platelets
- Fibrin threads

DRAW IT!

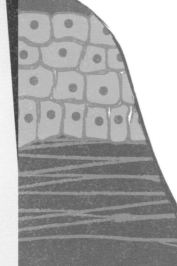
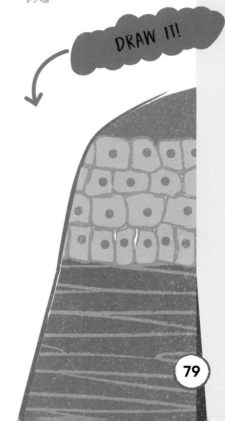

HUMAN BODY QUIZ

Now, it's time to test how much you've learned about the human body by taking this quiz. You can go back to earlier pages to look for clues and check up on some of the facts, if you need to. Good luck!

HOW DID YOU DO?

Once you have answered all the questions, you can check the answers on page 95. How many did you get right?

12–16 Wow! You're a budding doctor!

6–11 You're nearly qualified!

0–5 Return to medical school and have another go!

1 Which of these joints is a ball-and-socket joint?

a Shoulder
b Knee
c Thumb
d Elbow

2 Label the two types of cells in this diagram of a wound.

.... a

.... b

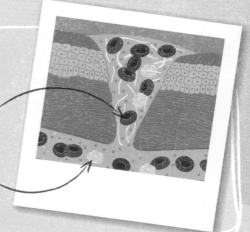

3 Whatever your eyes see is turned upside down on the retina at the back of the eye.

☐ True
☐ False

4 What is the gluteus maximus?

a The first Roman emperor
b A layer of your skin
c A large muscle in your bottom
d A place in Italy

5 We measure how loud or quiet a sound is on a scale. What is that scale called?

a Annabel scale
b Dingly Dell scale
c Decker scale
d Decibel scale

6 The male reproductive cell is called a sperm, and the female reproductive cell is called an oven.

☐ True   ☐ False

7 The largest artery in your body is called the aorta.

☐ True   ☐ False

8 The nucleus of each cell contains DNA, which contains instructions for life and tells the cell what to do. What does DNA stand for?

a Deoxyribonucleic acid
b Deoxygenated acid
c Decides new action
d Decidedly nasty acid

9 Our diet must include fiber. Why?

a For energy
b To keep our digestive system working properly
c To help us pass tests at school
d To help knit a sweater

10 Rapid Eye Movement (REM) sleep is when we don't dream.

☐ True   ☐ False

11 Your heart pumps blood rich in oxygen to the body. When it returns, the heart sends it to your lungs to pick up more oxygen. Can you label the **heart** and **lungs** in this picture of the body's circulatory system?

a ....
b ....

13 During which life stage does puberty take place?

a Childhood
b Adolescence
c Adulthood
d Old age

12 You have 206 bones in your body, and more than half of them are in your hands and feet.

☐ True   ☐ False

14 Which of these is NOT a reflex action by your nervous system (one that happens automatically)?

a Blinking
b Dilation of your pupils
c Gagging
d Picking up an apple

16 A human pregnancy lasts about 9 months and is split into trimesters. How many trimesters are there?

a One
b Two
c Three
d Four

15 Which one of these is a nerve cell?

a ☐   b ☐   c ☐   d ☐

THE BODY IN ACTION

Your body is busy working night and day. When you exercise, your heart, lungs, muscles, and senses work even harder. In fact, regular exercise benefits all of your bodily systems, even your digestion!

COLOR IT!

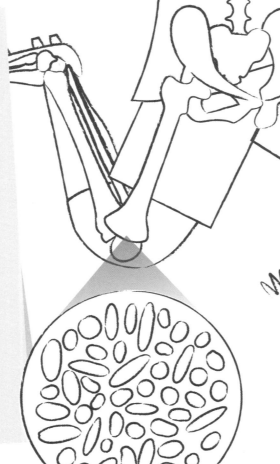

COLOR IT!

Color the body parts listed below. (Return to earlier pages if you need to refresh your memory.) Then, color the rest of the scene however you like.

Coloring key

- Brain
- Heart
- Stomach
- Humerus
- Hamstrings
- Iris
- Pupil
- Red blood cells
- White blood cells
- Platelets
- Bone marrow

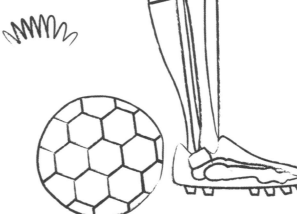

AMAZING BODY FACTS

One thing you are sure to have learned by this point in the book is that your body is pretty amazing! Here are some more body facts to astound you...

How many?
On both the inside and outside of your body are many cells (and bacteria) that can only be seen with a microscope.

NUMBER OF BACTERIA IN AN AVERAGE POO
10 TRILLION

NUMBER OF NEURONS IN THE HUMAN BRAIN
86 BILLION

NUMBER OF SWEAT PORES IN YOUR SKIN
2.5 MILLION

NUMBER OF LIGHT RECEPTORS IN THE HUMAN EYE
126 MILLION

NUMBER OF TASTE BUDS ON YOUR TONGUE
10,000

Per day

During one day, without even exercising, your body makes, loses, and recycles fluids all over the place.

half a pint (0.25 liter)
How much water you breathe out in droplets

1 quart (1 liter)
How much sweat your skin produces

1.5 quarts (1.4 liters)
How much urine (pee) your body makes

2 quarts (2 liters)
How much slimy mucus your lungs produce

3 quarts (3 liters)
How much digestive juice your stomach makes

48 gallons (180 liters)
How much blood your kidneys filter

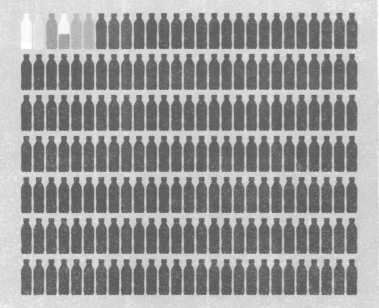

Lifetime achievement awards

If you live to be 80 years old, you'll be eligible to receive all of these prestigious awards.

220 million steps

Walking
You'll have walked about four times around the world.

500 bathtubs

Making spit
Your mouth will have made enough saliva to fill 500 bathtubs!

11 ft (3.4 m)

Nail-growing
If you never cut them, each fingernail would be 11 ft (3.4 m) long.

4.5 years

Eating
In total, you'll have devoted approximately 4.5 years of your life to eating.

80 days

Tooth-brushing
About 80 days of your life will have been spent brushing your teeth.

100 days

Pooing
You will have spent about 100 days of your life having a poo!

Biggest, smallest, fastest…

Here's a small snapshot of how remarkable your body is—from the tiny bone that translates sound waves into brain signals to the large muscles that enable humans to stand upright.

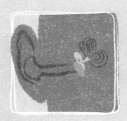

Smallest bone
The tiny, stirrup-shaped stapes bone in your middle ear is 0.1 in (3 mm)—the size of a sesame seed!

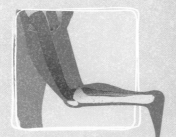

Longest bone
Your femur (thigh bone) grows to about 17 in (45 cm) and is where lots of blood cells are made.

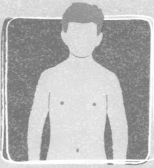

Biggest organ
Most of your organs are on the inside, but your largest organ is on the outside—your skin!

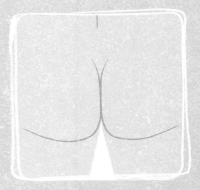

Biggest muscle
The gluteus maximus in your bottom is the largest muscle. After all, it helps you walk and stand up.

Strongest muscle
The masseter (the muscle that closes your jaw) can exert a bite force of 265 lb (120 kg).

Strongest tendon
Your Achilles tendon, which attaches your calf to your heel, can resist a force of 900 lb (400 kg).

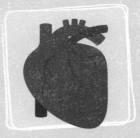

Hardest-working muscles
The muscles in your heart never rest. On average, they contract 60 times a minute for your whole life.

Fastest muscles
The orbicularis oculi muscles that make your eyes blink can contract in 1/100th of a second.

How long do cells last?

Some cells last a lifetime, while others die after just a few days and have to be replaced. Cells in hard-working parts of the body, such as the lining of the intestines, have the shortest life-spans.

Gut lining cells
These cells must be replaced constantly to protect your gut.

Outer skin cells
Every minute, you lose 30,000–40,000 dead skin cells.

Red blood cells
When these busy cells die, they are recycled in your liver.

Egg cells
Female egg cells are there at birth and last about 50 years.

TIME

| 3 DAYS | 10 DAYS | 1 MONTH | 2 MONTHS | 4 MONTHS | 8 YEARS | 50 YEARS | LIFETIME |

Taste bud cells
These hardworking cells need to be renewed regularly.

Sperm
These short-lived cells are produced in the male testes.

Fat cells
Each fat cell can shrink and grow in size during this time.

Nerve cells
These long-lived cells really are "made for life"!

GLOSSARY

Abundant
Something that there is lots of

Amplify
Make louder

Antibody
A special protein made by white blood cells to attack foreign substances, such as germs, that have infected the body

Artery
A blood vessel that takes blood away from the heart to other parts of the body

Bacteria
A group of tiny, single-celled organisms, some of which can cause disease or infection

Blood vessel
A tube through which blood travels

Bone marrow
A jellylike substance found in the center of most bones

Braille
A system of writing for blind people; the letters are printed as groups of raised dots that you can feel with your fingers.

Capillary
The smallest type of blood vessel, which takes blood to the body's cells and connects arteries to veins

Cardiac
Relating to the heart

Cartilage
Tough, flexible tissue in the nose, ears, ends of bones, and ribs; it helps the smooth, frictionless movement of joints.

Cells
The smallest units that make up a living thing

Clone
To make an identical copy of something

Concave
Curving inward

Convex
Curving outward

Cross-section
What you see when you cut through the middle of something, so that you can see the different layers it is made of

Decipher
Figure out, decode, or solve

Dense
Very heavy in relation to its size

Differentiate
Recognize or show the differences between two things

Digestion
The process in the digestive system that breaks down food to be used by the body

Dilate
Become larger, wider, or more open

DNA
The chemical found in body cells that determines how every cell will grow and function

Donor
Someone who gives blood or a part of their body to be used by another person who is ill

Embed
To place something firmly and deeply in a substance or solid object

Embryo
The earliest stage of a baby's development in the womb, before it is eight weeks old

Enzyme
A special protein created by the body to help speed up processes, such as breaking down food in the digestion process

Esophagus
The long tube that carries food from the mouth to the stomach

Facial
Relating to the face

Fertilization
When the egg and sperm join to produce an embryo

Fetus
The developing baby inside the womb, after it is eight weeks old

Flex
To bend, move, or stretch an arm or a leg or to pull a muscle tight

Genes
Sections of DNA that carry instructions for how the body is made up; genes are passed from parents to children.

Gland
A small organ that releases such substances as sweat, hormones, tears, or saliva

Hormone
A chemical made by a gland and released into the bloodstream, which sends a message to another part of the body

Inverted
Turned inside out or upside down

Iris
The round, colored part of a person's eye that surrounds the pupil

Ligament
A band of strong tissue that connects bones

Lobe
A rounded section of an organ; for example, the brain has four main lobes.

Mature
To become fully developed

Membrane
A thin, flexible structure that acts as a lining or covering

Metabolize
A chemical process that turns food, minerals, and so forth in the body into new cells, energy, and waste products

Microscopic
Extremely small, difficult or impossible to see without a microscope

Molecule
A tiny particle of a substance

Mucus
A slimy fluid produced in parts of the body, such as the nose, lungs, throat, and stomach, for protection or to allow something to move easily

Nerve
A fiber that carries electrical messages to and from the brain

Neuron
A nerve cell that sends and receives electrical signals to pass messages through the nervous system

Nourish
To provide a person, animal, or plant with the food that is necessary for life, growth, and good health

Nucleus
The central part of a cell that tells it what to do

Nutrients
Substances in food that the body needs for energy, growth, health, and cell repair

Organ
A part of the body made of tissues that work together to do a particular job; examples include the heart, liver, and eyes.

Particle
A tiny portion of matter

Pore
A tiny opening in the skin through which sweat can pass

Proprioception
The body's sense of where our limbs and body are in space

Protein
An organic substance made from nutrients that is an essential part of all living organisms

Puberty
The period when changes occur in the body as a child starts to develop into a young adult

Pupil
The dark, circular opening in the center of the front of the eye

Receptor
A part of a cell that picks up sensory information, such as light, heat, or pain, and passes the information on as signals in a nerve

Reflex
An automatic reaction that is beyond your control; for example, blinking

Regulate
To control an activity or process

Replicate
To make an exact copy of something

Reproduction
The biological process by which an animal or plant produces offspring (babies)

Saliva
A clear liquid made in the mouth by glands to help digest food

Skeleton
The framework of bones that supports the body

Spherical
Round like a ball

Stimulus
Something that produces a reaction or activity

Tendon
Toughened connective tissue that connects muscles to bones

Thrive
To become, and continue to be, successful, healthy, or strong

Tissue
A group of cells in the body that all carry out similar jobs

Toxic
Harmful, poisonous, and potentially deadly

Transparent
See-through

Trillion
One million million (1,000,000,000,000)

Vein
A blood vessel that carries blood to the heart from other parts of the body

Vertebra
One of the small bones running down your back from the neck to the pelvis, which are linked to form the spine

Vertical
Standing or pointing straight up

Vibration
Repeated small, quick shaking movements that produce a quivering effect or sound

X-ray
A high-energy form of electromagnetic radiation that is used to produce photographic images of bones

ANSWERS

4-5 BUILDING BLOCKS

LABEL THE BODY PARTS
a Organ system
b Tissue
c Cell
d Organ

MATCH THE CELL TYPES
a Red blood cell
b Intestine cell
c Muscle cell
d Fat cell
e Nerve cell
f White blood cell

6-7 SUPPORTIVE SKELETON

COMPLETE THE SKELETON

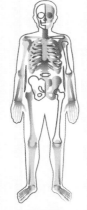

LABEL THE BONES
a Clavicle
b Humerus
c Rib
d Vertebra
e Femur

UNSCRAMBLE THE WORD
Femur

WHAT CAN YOU SEE?
Skull, Ribs, Pelvis

8-9 INSIDE A BONE

MATCH THE STAGES
a Embryo
b Newborn baby
c Child
d Teenager
e Adult

COLOR THE BONE

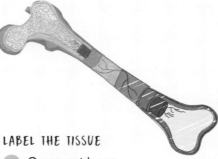

LABEL THE TISSUE
a Compact bone
b Spongy bone
c Red bone marrow

DECODE IT!
Blood cells

10-11 JOINTS

FIND THE JOINTS

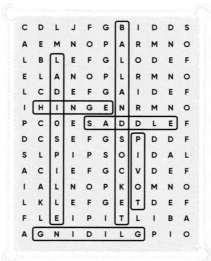

TAKE A LOOK INSIDE

WHICH IS WHICH?
a Pivot joint
b Hinge joint
c Ellipsoidal joint
d Saddle joint
e Ball-and-socket joint
f Gliding joint

12-13 MUSCLE POWER

WHICH IS WHICH?

a Skeletal muscle

b Cardiac muscle

c Smooth muscle

FIND THE MISSING MUSCLES

LABEL IT

a Triceps
b Pectoralis major
c Rectus abdominis
d Quadriceps
e Gluteus maximus
f Hamstrings

WHERE IS THE MUSCLE?

On your bottom

14-15 FLEXING YOUR MUSCLES

LABEL THE MUSCLES

a Temporalis
b Orbicularis oculi
c Zygomaticus major
d Masseter
e Orbicularis oris

FLEXING OR RESTING?

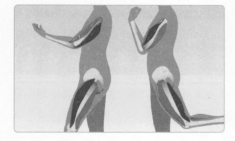

WORK IT OUT!

Seven

16-17 THE NERVOUS SYSTEM

WORK OUT THE STAGES

Left to right: 1, 2, 3, 4, 5

FOLLOW THE SIGNALS

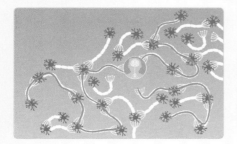

MATCH THE MOVEMENTS

a Knee-jerk
b Pupils dilate
c Blink
d Gag

18-19 THE BRAIN

UNSCRAMBLE IT!

Parietal lobe

MAKE THE CONNECTION

a Gray matter
b White matter
c Corpus callosum

THINK ABOUT THIS!

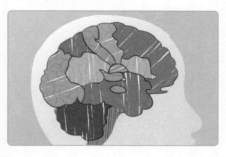

WHICH IS WHICH?

a PET   b MRA   c MRI

20-21 THE VOICE

FIND YOUR VOICE

a Shouting
b Singing
c Chatting
d Laughing

FIND THE WORDS

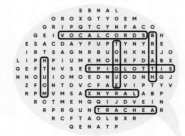

WHAT ARE YOU SAYING?

a "Ee"
b "Oo"
c "Ah"

WHICH IS WHICH?

a Breathing
b Speaking

22-23 SENSES

MAKE SENSE OF THE WORLD

Here's what ours look like!

Feel it!

Breathe it in

What a view!

Can you hear it?

Full of flavor

Keep on moving

DON'T THINK ABOUT IT (our examples)

a Walking in a straight line
b Kicking a ball without looking
c Reaching for objects

REVEAL THE WORD

Receptors

TRUE OR FALSE?

a True
b False
c True
d False

MAKE SENSE OF IT!

a Fine details and texture
b Pain or injury
c Light touch and vibrations

DRAW YOURSELF

Here's what ours looks like!

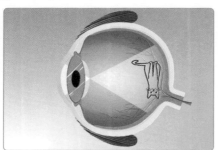

26-27 **THE EYE**

FILL IN THE BLANKS

a Lens
b Cornea
c Pupil
d Iris
e Sclera
f Retina
g Optic nerve

FLIP THE CAT / INSPECT YOUR IRIS

In this example, the person has green eyes.

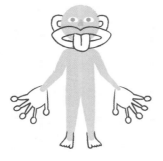

WHICH IS WHICH?

a Large pupil
b Small pupil
c Medium pupil

UNSCRAMBLE THE EYE CHARTS

a Retina
b Cornea
c Pupil
d Sclera

28-29 **SEEING THINGS**

WHAT DO YOU SEE?

a Parallel
b They are the same
c Both

WHICH LENS?

a Convex
b Concave

FIND THE NUMBERS

a 8
b 13
c 7

30-31 **HEARING**

COLOR ME IN

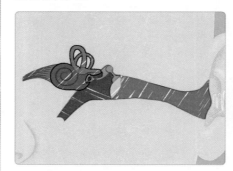

WHICH IS WHICH?

a Inner ear
b Middle ear
c Outer ear

HOW LOUD?

Here's what ours looks like!

a

Leaves rustling

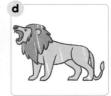
b

Rainfall

c

City traffic

d

Lion's roar

e

Blue whale song

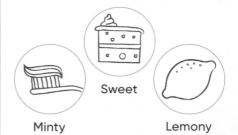
f

Space shuttle blast-off

32-33 **SMELL**

WHAT'S THAT SMELL?

We chose these objects!

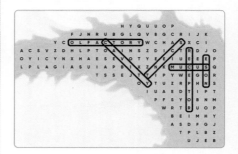

Minty

Sweet

Lemony

FIND THE WORDS

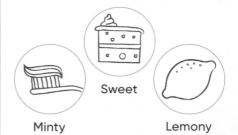

CRACK THE NOSE CODE

Anosmia

34-35 TASTE

FIND THE WORDS

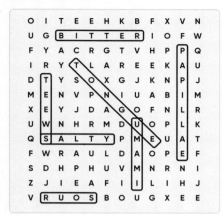

COLOR THE TASTE BUD

REVEAL THE SUPERTASTER

a. Normal taster

b. Supertaster

SOLVE THE TASTE-OKU

36-37 BREATHING

IN OR OUT?

a. Breathing in

b. Breathing out

FINISH THE PICTURE

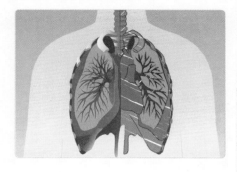

UNSCRAMBLE IT

Carbon dioxide

HOW MANY BREATHS?

a. Over 18 years old

b. 1–3 years old

c. 6–12 years old

38-39 THE CIRCULATORY SYSTEM

FILL IN THE OXYGEN LOOPS

a. Lungs

b. Body

MATCH THE BLOOD VESSELS

a. Artery

b. Capillary

c. Vein

NAME THE PARTS

a. Lungs

b. Heart

c. Arteries

d. Veins

e. Capillaries

IDENTIFY THE WORD

Capillaries

40-41 THE HEART

DECIPHER THE HEART PARTS

a. Aorta

b. Atrium

c. Ventricle

d. Valve

e. Artery

FIND YOUR PULSE

Patient A: Regular

Patient B: Irregular

WHAT IS THE HEART DOING?

a. Push

b. Relax

c. Squeeze

42-43 IN THE BLOOD

MATCH THE CELLS

a. Plasma

b. White blood cells

c. Platelets

d. Red blood cells

WHO CAN HAVE THE BLOOD?

Blood O: O, A, B, and AB

Blood A: A and AB

Blood B: B and AB

Blood AB: AB

COLOR THE LAYERS

44-45 THE URINARY SYSTEM

UNSCRAMBLE THEM
a Kidneys
b Ureter
c Bladder
d Nephrons
e Urethra

COLOR THE KIDNEY

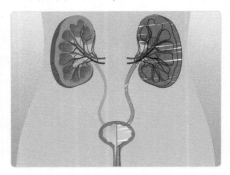

FILTER THE BLOOD
Process from start: 1, 2, 3, 4, 5

WHAT IS URINE MADE OF?

46-47 THE DIGESTIVE SYSTEM

SPOT THE DIFFERENCE

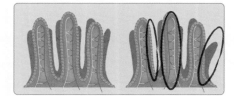

QUIZ YOURSELF!
a Break down food
b Small intestine
c Nutrients
d At least 24 hours

DO THE MATH!

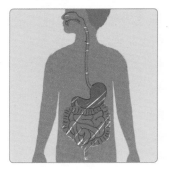

WHICH IS WHICH?
a Leaving
b Digesting
c Swallowing
d Absorbing

48-49 TALES OF YOUR TEETH

LABEL THE PARTS
a Enamel
b Dentine
c Pulp
d Blood vessels
e Gums
f Jawbone

DO THE TEETH-OKU

IDENTIFY THE TEETH
a Grip and grind
b Crush and grind
c Cut
d Tear

WHICH ARE WHICH?

50-51 GUT REACTIONS

FINISH THE ZOOM-IN

HOW MANY DRINKS?

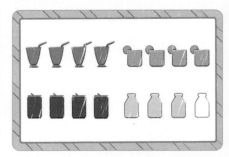

HOW ACIDIC IS STOMACH ACID?
Between 1.5 and 3.5

52-53 NUTRITION

FILL YOUR PLATE
Here's the food we chose for a balanced meal in China:

DECODE THE MESSAGE
Drinking orange juice with your beans helps you absorb their iron.

SORT LIFE'S ESSENTIALS

a Fiber
b Vitamins
c Minerals
d Lipids
e Carbohydrates
f Protein

54-55 THE LIVER

FINISH THE PICTURE

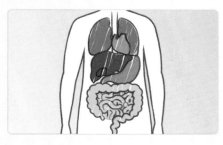

COLOR THE COGS

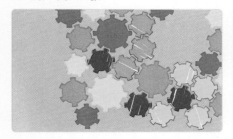

WHICH IS WHICH?

a Liver
b Small intestine
c Gallbladder
d Heart

56-57 SKIN, HAIR, AND NAILS

LOOK UNDER YOUR SKIN

HOW ABOUT YOU?

We chose this type of hair!

LABEL THE NAIL

a Nail
b Nail bed
c Cuticle
d Nail root

WHICH IS WHICH?

a New growth
b Active follicle
c Resting stage

58-59 THE MALE REPRODUCTIVE SYSTEM

A SPERM'S JOURNEY

a Seminal vesicle
b Sperm duct
c Penis
d Urethra
e Epididymis

SPOT THE CHANGES

a Facial and body hair
b Growth and strength
c Voice

60-61 THE FEMALE REPRODUCTIVE SYSTEM

AN EGG'S JOURNEY

a Egg
b Fallopian tube
c Ovary
d Uterus

WHAT ARE PERIODS?

Days 19-28: The lining is ready
Days 11-18: Ovulation
Days 7-10: An egg develops
Days 1-6: A period

62-63 PREGNANCY

WHICH SPERM?

The blue sperm reaches the egg.

COLOR BY NUMBER

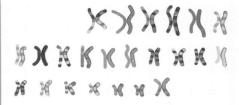

64-65 INSTRUCTIONS FOR LIFE

COLOR THE PAIRS

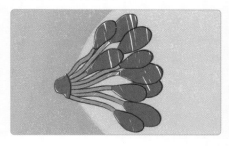

COMPLETE THE BASES

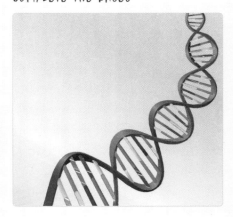

CRACK THE CODE

An uncurled DNA strand is two meters long.

66-67 GROWING UP

WHICH STAGE IS WHICH?

1 Rolling along
2 First steps
3 School time
4 All change
5 All grown up
6 Slowing down

DRAW YOURSELF
Here's what ours looks like!

As a baby

Now

At 40 years old

At 80 years old

UNSCRAMBLE THE LIFE STAGE
Puberty

68-69 THE ENDOCRINE SYSTEM

WHICH IS WHICH?

a

Insulin

b

Adrenaline

c

Estrogen

d

Thyroxine

HOW DO WE KNOW WHEN TO SLEEP?
At dusk: Melatonin
At dawn: Serotonin
Mid-morning: Cortisol

FIND THE WORDS

DECODE IT!
Somatotropin

70-71 SLEEP

WHICH IS WHICH?

Theta waves

Alpha waves

Delta waves

Beta waves

HOW MUCH SLEEP DO YOU NEED?

a 16 hours
b 10 hours
c 8 hours
d 7 hours

DRAW YOUR LAST DREAM
This happened in our last dream!

72-73 VIRUS INVASION

SPOT THE IMPOSTER!

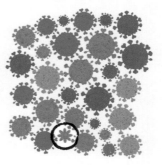

WHICH IS WHICH?

a Helical
b Complex
c Polyhedral
d Enveloped

ATTACK THE CELLS

Enveloped

Polyhedral

Helical

Complex

FIND THE RIGHT VACCINE

a Vaccine

74-75 BACTERIA

WHICH IS WHICH?

a Vibrio

b Spirillum

c Spirochaeta

d Coccus

e Bacillus

COMPLETE IT!

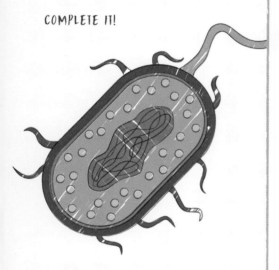

DO THE MATH!
1928

MATCH THE ANTIBIOTICS!

a 4

b 3

c 1

d 2

76-77 THE IMMUNE SYSTEM

NAME THAT CELL
Phagocyte

SOLVE THE RIDDLE
I look like the letter Y

TRACK A GERM'S JOURNEY

b Germ

d Antibody

c Clones

a Phagocyte

78-79 HEALING

FIND THE HEALING WORDS!

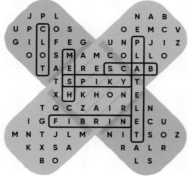

FILL IT IN

a Fracture

b Callus

c New bone grows

d Healed bone

HEAL THE CUT!

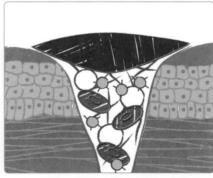

80-81 HUMAN BODY QUIZ

1 a. Shoulder

2 a. Red blood cell

   b. White blood cell

3 True

4 c. A large muscle in your bottom

5 d. Decibel scale

6 False (the female cell is AN OVUM)

7 True

8 a. Deoxyribonucleic acid

9 b. To keep our digestive system working properly

10 False (REM is when we DO dream)

11 a. Heart

    b. Lungs

12 True

13 b. Adolescence

14 d. Picking up an apple

15 d

16 c. Three

82-83 THE BODY IN ACTION

DRAW YOUR OWN!
Here's what ours looks like!

INDEX

ACKNOWLEDGMENTS

DK would like to thank the following for their help with this book: Catharine Robertson for proofreading; Elizabeth Wise for compiling the index; Rona Skene and Elizabeth Blakemore for editorial assistance; Phil Gamble and Gus Scott for additional illustrations; Laura Gardner for additional jacket design.

DK would like to thank the following for their kind permission to reproduce their photographs:

(Key: a-above; b-below/bottom; c-center; f-far; l-left; r-right; t-top)

6 Dreamstime.com: Puwadol Jaturawutthichai (cla).
7 Dreamstime.com: Daboost (clb); Puwadol Jaturawutthichai (cb, crb). **8 Science Photo Library:** Power And Syred (crb). **9 Getty Images:** Brand X Pictures / Science Photo Library - STEVE GSCHMEISSNER. (clb). **Science Photo Library:** Steve Gschmeissner (cb). **19 Science Photo Library:** Centre Jean Perrin / ISM (clb); Living Art Enterprises, LLC (cb); Rajaaisya (crb). **21 123RF.com:** Kian Khoon Tan (cra). **22 Getty Images / iStock:** E+ / alle12 (cl). **24 Dreamstime. com:** Aleksey Eremeev (cl). **29 Dreamstime.com:** Eveleen007 (crb). **46 Science Photo Library:** Sebastian Kaulitzki (bl). **56 Shutterstock. com:** Prostock-studio (tr). **58 123RF.com:** stillfx. **60 123RF.com:** stillfx. **71 Getty Images / iStock:** kdshutterman (clb). **72 Dreamstime.com:** Kateryna Kon (crb)

All other images © Dorling Kindersley